FRENCH AND INDIANS
OF ILLINOIS RIVER

Shawnee Classics
A Series of Classic Regional Reprints for the Midwest

FRENCH
AND
INDIANS
OF
ILLINOIS
RIVER

Nehemiah Matson

With a New Foreword by Rodney O. Davis

Southern Illinois University Press
Carbondale and Edwardsville

The publisher gratefully acknowledges the cooperation of Lovejoy
Library, Southern Illinois University Edwardsville, in providing the
text of *French and Indians of Illinois River* that was used for the
present edition.

Library of Congress Cataloging-in-Publication Data

Matson, N. (Nehemiah), 1816–1883.
   French and Indians of Illinois River / Nehemiah
Matson ; with a new foreword by Rodney O. Davis.
      p. cm. — (Shawnee classics)
   Originally published: Princeton, Ill.: Republican Job Print.
      Establishment, 1874.
   Includes bibliographical references.
      1. Illinois—History—To 1778. 2. Indians of North America—
   Illinois—History. 3. French—Illinois—History. 4. Illinois River
   Valley (Ill.)—History. I. Title. II. Series.

F544 .M43 2001
977.3'5—dc21   00-030812
ISBN 0-8093-2364-8 (alk. paper)

The paper used in this publication meets the minimum requirements
of American National Standard for Information Sciences—Perma-
nence of Paper for Printed Library Materials, ANSI Z39.48-1992.∞

FOREWORD.

As both observer and participant in the frontier process, Nehemiah Matson (1816–1873) was a paradox. At the same time that he celebrated the occupation of the Middle West by European pioneers, he also labored to preserve the memory of the natives whom these same pioneers had necessarily, in his view, displaced. He prospered so much from the selling of land in northern Illinois to incoming settlers, land from which the very Indians whose record he desired to perpetuate had so lately been driven, that before he was fifty years old, he could describe himself occupationally as a "gentleman" and not long after, he could indulge himself in an eleven-month

grand tour of Europe and the Middle East. In Princeton, Illinois, his home community after 1836, he left behind as a worthy monument what became a handsome prairie style public library, partially endowed by him, named for him, and finally completed in 1913. His other major benefaction, of equal significance in his own eyes, consisted of the five books he authored on northern Illinois and Illinois River history and cartography, volumes based not only on conscientious scholarship but also on both Indian and white reminiscence and on local folklore. He left yet another book that was an account of his overseas trip and still another best described as fiction. The present volume is the second of Matson's local histories.[1]

To state matters succinctly, during much of his life, Nehemiah Matson combined the attributes of the scholar with those of the salesman and promoter. A lifelong concern of his was the inventorying of both the resources and the traditions of the town of Princeton and surrounding Bureau County. After migrating to Illinois as a youth from Ohio with his parents, he seems to have started adult life as a farmer, but he soon took up surveying. As a surveyor, he was among the first of the early white inhabitants to learn the topography and landscape of his environment intimately, and he could and did personally profit from that superior knowledge by taking up lands on his own hook for resale. "In those early times," according to a later local writer, "he gave much attention to the entering of lands for the incoming settlers, and soon became so familiar with the geography of the country that his services were in great demand. Always careful and painstaking, the people came to regard him as a standard authority on all land matters," as both consultant and salesman, obviously.[2] For the benefit of those who were curious about the climate of Bureau County, Matson kept and routinely published local meteorological observations, and in 1867, he commissioned the publication of a remarkably meticulous set of topographical maps of the county and its township, based on his own early surveys and on more recent ones that he sponsored. The volume in which the maps are contained is both local publicity brochure and a piece of respectable scholarship, and in each way it reveals some major preoccupations of Nehemiah Matson.[3]

But clearly the publications for which Matson most desired to be remembered were not maps or travel accounts but his local histories. Their origins seem to lie in the occasional presence of migrating Pottawatomie in the Bureau County of his youth, in the stories that he collected from them and from the earliest whites to succeed them, and in the legends, substantiatable or not, that had grown up in the neighborhood of Starved Rock and down the Illinois River. As a youth of twenty, having just arrived in Bureau County, the fascinated Matson conducted several lengthy interviews with Shaubena, the Pottawatomie chief regarded a renegade by his own people but as a friend to the white settlers during the recent Black Hawk War. Interests such as these only broadened over the years as Matson collected other tales from English-speaking and French-speaking settlers and traders or their descendants and conducted omnivorous reading of his own in the available published sources. And these interests were given even further depth by Matson's surveyor's knowledge of the landscape of his home area. He had been over the terrain himself and had known much of it in its pristine state. By the early 1870s, his leisure allowed him to write, to publish, and frequently to revise. The present volume is an example: first published in 1874, it is a reprint of the second edition of the book; the first edition was published earlier the same year, circulated among knowledgeable readers of his selection, and then corrected, undoubtedly at considerable expense to Matson, who had a surveyor's determination to get things right.

And it would appear that Matson's motive for publishing these local histories was quite different from that underlying his map project or his involvement in other local promotional efforts. He claimed to desire neither profit nor emulation. In his words, "the necessarily limited circulation [of his local histories] would prevent the former, and the criticisms common to local publications the latter." Instead, he professed an obligation. What he desired was simply to preserve the early history, indeed some of the prehistory, of the area. "The testimony of many of the early settlers, who are now in their graves, as well as of Indians that have long since passed away, was alone in the possession of the writer, and justice required that it should be given to the public. . . . The labors of the writer may not at present be appreciated, but the time will come when these facts, though crudely expressed, will be regarded of great importance, forming as they do the connecting link of history between the past, present, and future."[4] And in his time and for some time after, Matson's historical works were indeed considered authoritative and objects of emulation and considerable esteem.[5]

In our own time, we can say of *French and Indians of Illinois River* that it is possessed of both the liabilities and the considerable virtues of nineteenth-century amateur local history, complicated by the fact that much of Matson's subject matter was quite remote in time. A good bit of the book covers material otherwise well known: the explorations and missionary activities of Marquette and other Jesuits, the expeditions and trading activities of LaSalle and Tonti, Pontiac's conspiracy, and Tecumseh's uprising and the chain of events it initiated, including the Fort Dearborn Massacre and Thomas Craig's disastrous raid on Peoria. What is unique here is Matson's own personal perspective and the material he provides on the basis of his own researches.

Certainly Matson's own collecting of stories and reminiscences preserved information that would otherwise have been simply irretrievable by later investigators, especially since many of his informants, both Indian or of European descent, were illiterate. In a way, he was conduct-

ing an oral history project, though the interval
between some of his early Indian interviews and
their actual commitment to publication was
rather lengthy. And reminiscences and tradi-
tional accounts, at first hand or more remote,
generate their own problems. In Matson's case,
a major one was the inconsistency of informants'
statements with one another. As he ruefully
admits, "Harmonizing all conflicting accounts
. . . has not been a success." The reader will note
several instances of such conflict, freely acknowledged by Matson.

However, in other respects, Matson remains
quite authoritative, as in his soliciting and drawing from recent Pottawatomie accounts at the
end of this volume. And where Matson had personally covered the ground that he describes,
he is also very effective. For example, his own
archaeological inspection of Starved Rock and
vicinity successfully validates his claim that it,
and not neighboring Buffalo Rock, was the original site of LaSalle's Fort St. Louis. His descrip-

tions of the Illinois valley landscape are in the romantic mode in which much nineteenth-century writing was cast, but they also reflect the disciplined assessment of a surveyor who knew well the terrain of his home county. In some other instances, where his authority might be less but his opinions nonetheless difficult to hide, Matson's distinctive point of view is dominating. His admiration of the Jesuit missionaries on occasion borders on idolatry; his preference for the Illinois Indians over other nations is obvious; his disgust at the destruction of Black Partridge's village by Governor Edwards's Illinois rangers is palpable. And Matson's account of the burning of Peoria by Craig and his party is greatly enlivened by his interview with Hypolite Pilette, one of the survivors, who years after the event could still profess only hatred for its perpetrators.

Besides his reconnaissances and information gathering in Illinois, Matson's more academic preparation for this volume was also conscientious and far reaching. He admits his reliance on the writings of Parkman and Sparks, but he did primary research of his own. He visited the Jesuit archives at Rouen while on his European trip and consulted, apparently in the original, some of the narratives that would later be published in the great collection *Jesuit Relations* that was compiled at the turn of the century.[6] But his researches in the end could only be as thorough as the sources available to him would allow, and as a result, there is factual material in this volume of which more recent scholarship would mandate correction or at least reconsideration.

An early example is Matson's indication, twice, that the Illinois Indians were possessed of horses in the 1680s. The current major authority on that tribe believes that to have been impossible in 1680 though perhaps a little more likely in the second instance noted, in 1684.[7] Possibly of greater import is Matson's assertion that Fort St. Louis, established at Starved Rock by LaSalle and Tonti in 1682, was maintained at that site until 1718, the same year that Tonti died there. It has been established more recently that because of a shortage of furs and of firewood, Fort St. Louis was moved from the Rock to the south end of Lake Peoria in 1692 and that Tonti, furthermore, died not in Illinois but on the Gulf, at Mobile, in 1704.[8] One set of the conflicting accounts that Matson could not reconcile concerns the site of the assassination of Pontiac, the great rebel Ottawa chief, in 1769, at the instigation of some Illinois Indians. Matson is at pains to place that event at a council of Pottawatomie, Ottawa, and Illinois near the present site of Joliet, though he acknowledges that others assert that it took place at Cahokia on the Mississippi, two years earlier. Howard Peckham's work on Pontiac's rebellion is now considered definitive. Its author persuasively argues the latter location, with the killing taking place in 1769, the year Matson asserts.[9] Matson also retells the legend of the origin of the name of Starved Rock, according to which a large band of Illinois, fleeing from vengeful

Ottawa and Pottawatomie after Pontiac's death, were held under siege there. Others, beginning with Clarence Alvord years ago, have found no evidence of unusual intertribal warfare following the assassination.[10] Finally, Matson identifies Jean Baptiste duSable, probably the first permanent non-Indian resident at the site of Chicago, as a runaway slave from Kentucky whose thwarted major aspiration was to become a leader of the local Pottawatomie. DuSable is now understood to have originated in Santo Domingo and to have had no political aspirations to speak of. Instead, he was a successful Indian trader whose business and domestic establishments were most impressive for the time and place.[11]

Though contemporary readers ought to be conscious of such discrepancies as these, to stress them seems almost a disservice to so conscientious and committed an author as Nehemiah Matson. Obviously this book must be evaluated as what it is, a piece of colorful local history, romantically anchored in legend yet rooted also in invaluable research and produced by a dedicated amateur whose standards were high. The handicaps under which he labored were noted by contemporary admirers and still deserve acknowledgment.[12] And had Matson not contacted some of the informants that he did, their stories would never have been told. Thus, *French and Indians of Illinois River* is a model of its type, indeed a minor classic, and it richly deserves this return to a wider audience.

RODNEY O. DAVIS

NOTES

1. See Ruth Ewers Haberhorn, "Nehemiah Matson: Historian of Northern Illinois," *Journal of the Illinois State Historical Society* 53 (1960): 149–62; H. C. Bradsby, ed., *History of Bureau County, Illinois* (Chicago, 1885), 583. Matson dubbed himself a "gentleman" for the census-taker in 1860 (U.S. Eighth Census, 1860, Population Schedules for Bureau County, Illinois). At other times, he identified himself as a dealer in real estate (*Sketches of the Early Settlement and Present Advantages of Princeton . . . and a Business Directory* [Princeton, 1857] 34) and as an "author and traveller" (U.S. Ninth Census, 1870, Population Schedules for Bureau County, Illinois). His

travel account is *Beyond the Atlantic: Or Eleven Months Tour in Europe, Egypt and Palestine, with Illustrations* (Princeton, Illinois, 1870).

2. Pauline Schenk, *The Story of the Matson Public Library* ([Princeton,] 1927), 1.

3. *Map of Bureau County, Illinois, with Sketches of Its Early Settlement* (Chicago, 1867). See also *Sketches of the Early Settlement and Present Advantages of Princeton*, 41, for Matson's meteorological table for Princeton.

4. Nehemiah Matson, *Reminiscences of Bureau County* (Princeton, 1872), 10.

5. Bradsby's *History of Bureau County, Illinois* relies heavily on Matson, and Matson's work is cited respectfully in Newton Bateman and Paul Selby, eds., *Historical Encyclopedia of Illinois* (Chicago, 1894). See, for example, p. 427.

6. Reuben Gold Thwaites, ed., *The Jesuit Relations and Allied Documents: Travels and Explorations of the Jesuit Missionaries in New France, 1610–1791*, 73 vols. (Cleveland, 1896–1901).

7. Raymond Houser to Rodney O. Davis, interview, March 19, 1998.

8. Clarence W. Alvord, *The Illinois Country, 1673–1848* (Springfield, 1920), 100, 110; Edmund Robert Murphy, *Henry de Tonty: Fur Trader of the Mississippi* (Baltimore, 1941), 67–68, 84.

9. Howard H. Peckham, *Pontiac and the Indian Uprising* (Princeton, 1947), 310–11.

10. Alvord, 273n; Peckham, 316.

11. Bessie Louise Pierce, *A History of Chicago* (Chicago, 1937), 1, 12–13; Thomas A. Meehan, "Jean Baptiste du Sable, the First Chicagoan," *Journal of the Illinois State Historical Society* 56 (1963): 439–53.

12. Bradsby, 583; E. K. Mercer, in a paper read at the dedication of the library named for Matson, May 9, 1913, Nehemiah Matson Collection, Matson Public Library, Princeton, Illinois.

INTRODUCTION.

The beautiful country between the Wabash and Mississippi rivers, now within the boundaries of the Sucker State, was once occupied by the powerful tribe of Illinois Indians. Over these prairies, and through these groves, these wild people, while in their native simplicity roamed at pleasure. Generation succeeded generation, and no one doubted their right to possess the land. The French came and lived among them, introducing a new religion with arts of civilization, and between the races harmony and friendship prevailed. But afterwards an enemy came, war and carnage followed, and the Illinoians were annihilated.

For a time the conquerors possessed the land, but the tide of civilization, which is ever rolling westward, compelled them to find a new home beyond the Father of Waters.

To give some account of these events, has been the object of this work, and to what extent these efforts have been a success, the reader is left to judge. Some of the incidents herein narrated, are drawn from history, others from traditions, while many are from the statements of persons who figured in them. To collect these traditions from the Indians and early French pioneers, has been the work of many years, and harmonizing all conflicting accounts, candor compels me to admit, has not been a success.

This is an account of people who left no history, and all that is known of them are scraps of tradition, which are more or less vailed in doubt and uncertainty. While the Indians were still in the country, I obtained from them many things relating to the past; some of which are confirmed by notes recently collected among the tribe in western Kansas.

The descendants of the early French pioneers now living on the American Bottom, have also been interviewed, and all their traditions carefully noted. Many of the places where marked events occurred have been visited; at some of which relics of the past still exist.

A short time since, a small edition of this work was published and copies of it sent among the descendants of the French pioneers, Fur Traders, Indian Agents, etc., for the purpose of obtaining their criticism; and through this means many errors were detected, and new facts developed.

This book does not claim to be a full and complete history of the French and Indians of the Illinois river, but will be found to consist mainly of sketches and incidents relating thereto. Neither does it vouch for the correctness of every statement made in its pages; as many of them are compiled from conflicting accounts, and of their probability or improbability, others can decide.

Among those who aided me in my researches were Geo. E. Walker and Col. Gerden S. Hubbard, of Chicago ; Col. D. F. Hitt and David Walker, of Ottawa ; John Hamlin, of Peoria, and Lyman C. Draper, of Madison, Wisconsin.

N. M.

PRINCETON, September 1, 1874.

CONTENTS.

CONTENTS.

CONTENTS.

FRENCH AND INDIANS
OF ILLINOIS RIVER

CHAPTER I.

On a clear warm day in the early part of September, 1673, two bark canoes were seen slowly gliding up the Illinois river, whose placid waters had never before reflected the face of a white man. These canoes were propelled up stream partly by sail and partly by oars, and as they went forward the travelers on board of them caused the wild woods along the shores to resound with songs of praise. On the sail of the foremost canoe was painted various devices, representing a coat of arms, a pipe of peace, and a cross—emblematical of power, friendship and Christianity.

The voyageurs were delighted with the country through which they were passing, and they made many comments on the beauty of the surrounding scenery. Large herds of buffalo were seen feeding on the prairie, and at the sound of the oars, elk, deer and antelope would arise from their lair, and bound away across the distant plains. Wild geese and swans were swimming in the river, while flocks of paroquets made merry the lonely waters with their songs.

This party of travelers consisted of nine persons. Louis Joliet, a government officer; Jacques Marquette, a Jesuit priest; five oarsmen, and two Indian interpreters. They were the first to discover the upper Mississippi, having descended it in their canoes from the mouth of Wisconsin river to its junction with Arkansas. Here they became satisfied that this great river of the west did not empty into the Pacific ocean, as they had supposed, but into the South Sea, consequently, they turned their canoes up stream, and were on their return to Canada to report the success of their discoveries.

It was late in the afternoon when the voyageurs arrived at LaVantum—the great town of Illinois —located on the north bank of the river, near the present site of Utica. They were surprised to find here a large town, built along the river bank for more than a mile in extent, while back of it the great meadow was covered with corn-fields, camping tents, and swarmed with human beings.

As the voyageurs approached the town, the Indians in great numbers collected on the river bank to see these strange people, never before having looked upon the face of a white man. Warriors, armed with bows and arrows, lined the

shore, prepared to give the strangers battle, if
enemies, and greet them with kindness, if friends.
The canoes came to a halt, when Joliet displayed
the "Wampum," (a token of friendship,) at the
sight of which the warriors lowered their weapons,
and motioned them to come ashore. On landing,
Father Marquette approached the Indians, while
holding aloft in one hand the pipe of peace, and
in the other a small gold cross. The Indians collected around Marquette, in great astonishment,
offering him many presents to appease the wrath
of the great Manito, from whom they believed
the strangers had come. The travelers left their
canoes, and were conducted to the lodge of the
head chief, Chassagoac, where they were kindly
entertained.

On the following day, at the request of Joliet,
all the Indians of the town were assembled on the
river bank, to hear the good tidings brought by
the strangers. Here Joliet planted a post, on
which he placed the portrait of Louis XIV,
together with a picture of the French coat of
arms. Around this post, seated on the ground,
were about one thousand warriors, while back of
them were standing many thousand squaws and
pappooses. When all was silent, Joliet advanced
toward the post, holding aloft in one hand his
sword, and in the other a sod of earth, proclaim-

ing in a loud voice, "In the name and by the
authority of the most high Christian King of
France, Louis XIV, I take possession of all the
country from Canada to the Pacific, and from the
Lakes to the South Sea, and henceforth it shall be
called New France." At this announcement, all
the Frenchmen fired their guns, and shouted
"*Vive le roi.*"

After completing this ceremony, Joliet addressed the Indians as follows: "On this post
you see the picture and coat of arms of the greatest chief on earth, whom we call King. He lives
across the big waters, and his domain extends
from sea to sea, and there is no chief like him in
all the world. People from all countries come to
take counsel of him and do his bidding. This
great chief will be your father, and you will be
his children ; he will supply you with beads,
knives, hatchets, &c., and he will protect you
from the attacks of your great enemies, the Iroquois." At the conclusion of Joliet's speech, the
Indians beat their drums, clapped their hands
and shouted with joy.

Father Marquette now came forward and un-
rolled a canvass, on which was painted a picture
of Christ nailed to the cross. Raising the canvass above his head, so all the warriors could see
the picture, he said, "This is the Savior of the

world, who died to redeem all mankind, and is the ruler of earth and sky." Again the Indians beat their drums, clapped their hands and shouted long and loud.

When order was restored, Marquette preached to the warriors, explaining to them the great importance of abandoning the religion of their fathers and embracing Christianity. Chassagoac the head chief, with many of his friends were converted under Marquette's preaching and baptized by him, as members of the Catholic church. Marquette gave the chief a number of mementoes consisting of crosses crucifixes, &c., which he kept about his person for more than fifty years, and at the time of his death they were buried with him.

On the third day the canoes of the travelers were again on the water, and on reaching Lake Michigan at the mouth of Chicago river, the party separated. Joliet with three companions, continued on his way to Canada to report his discovery to the Governor; while Marquette with two others, went to Green Bay for the purpose of converting the Indians.

As Joliet was passing down the rapids of St. Lawrence river, near Montreal, his canoe upset, and his journal with all other valuables, were lost.

These explorers published no account of their travels, and the world was but little wiser for their journey, except establishing the fact, that the Mississippi river did not flow into the Pacific ocean, and Illinois was a rich country.

STARVED ROCK.

On the south bank of the Illinois river, eight miles below Ottawa, and near the foot of the rapids, is a remarkable cliff known as Starved Rock. This rocky cliff rises almost perpendicular from the water's edge to the hight of one hundred and thirty-six feet, and is separated from neighboring cliffs by a wide chasm, which shows signs of having been produced by some convulsion of nature. Three sides of this rock rises like a watch-tower; but the fourth, next to the bluff, recedes inward, and at one place can be ascended by a steep rocky stair-like pathway. Among crevises in the rocks are stunted cedars, and between these the cactus and mountain ivy grow. The walls of this cliff are of gray sand-stone, partly hid with forest trees, and viewed from a distance has the appearance of an old castle of feudal times.

Starved Rock is of a circular form, and from every stand-point it has a bold, majestic appearance. On the north side, next to the river, the cliff is perpendicular, rising in towering masses, and, as it were, frowning down on the rapid stream which flows at its base. In some places the walls are smooth, and thick layers of rock look like the work of art, while at other places they are rough with overhanging crags, and under which are many dark, dismal-looking caverns, once the abode of wild animals.

A part of the summit of Starved Rock consists of smooth sand-stone, on which are engraved many names of visitors, but the larger portion of it is covered by earth, with grass and small trees growing thereon. The rock contains an area of about three-fourths of an acre, and abounds on all sides with shrubs of evergreens.

Here, by the side of the river stands this high, isolated rock, the same as it stood centuries ago, overlooking the broad valley below and the many wood-clad islands which divide the swift current of the Illinois, and here it will stand a monument of the past, and the admiration of the future. Its bold, towering walls ; its high, majestic summit, and its isolated position, makes it the most pictu- resque object on the Illinois river ; and for histori- cal interest it has no equal in the western country.

The view from the summit of Starved Rock is very fine, and the country in the distance will re- mind the beholder of a grand landscape painting or a beautiful panorama. To the north and west is seen a large bottom prairie, bounded on each side by bluffs covered with forest trees. Through this great meadow flows the Illinois river, which can be seen for many miles distant, winding about in its serpentine course. On looking down into the river at the base of the rock, catfish and turtles can be seen sporting over the sand and rocks in the clear shallow stream ; while shoals of red-horse are steming the swift current.

In the early settlement of the country, Starved Rock became a noted land-mark, visited generally by people traveling through the country, and by them it was regarded as a great natural curiosity.

Of latter years, it has become a place of resort for excursion and pic-nic parties from the neighboring cities, and no one ever visited it without being captivated with its wild romantic scenery.

By the early French explorers, Starved Rock was called Le Rocher, and through them it has figured extensively in the history of western discoveries. Almost two centuries ago La Salle built a fort on its summit, the remains of which are still to be seen ; and around this fort was clustered the first colony in the valley of the Mississippi.

Two hundred years has made but little alteration in the appearance of Starved Rock ; the same fort-like walls remain, and probably the same

stunted cedars crown its summit, but the surroundings have undergone a great change. The
great meadow which its summit overlooks, once
covered with grass and wild flowers, and sometimes blackened with herds of buffalo, is now
occupied by farms in close succession. To the
north, across the large bottom prairie is seen the
village of Utica, with its cement mills and ware-
houses, and by the side of which, pass the canal
and railroad. To the west, five miles below, but
in plain view are the flourishing cities of LaSalle
and Peru, with their church steeples glittering in
the sunbeams, while steam and canal boats are
seen in the river, and trains of cars passing and
repassing on the different railroads. Evidence of
agriculture, commerce and civilization are now
to be seen from the summit of Starved Rock,
where the scenery was once wild and lonely ; and
here, was also heard the wild war-whoop of
savages while engaged in the bloody strife, leaving the great meadow below strewn with dead,
the result of an Iroquois victory.

The summit of Starved Rock was, at one time
the abode of gay and joyous Frenchmen, where
balls and wine suppers were held ; and here, too,
was heard, morning and evening, the songs of
praise from the lips of devout Jesuit priests. At
another time it was a scene of strife, carnage and

desolation, stained with human blood, and covered with the bodies of the slain. Pleasure parties now dance on this rock, but they do not consider that here was once the dance of death—where the infant, the mother, the young maiden, the brave warrior, and the aged chief alike suffered and died.

No spot in the great west is so closely identified with the early history of the country as Starved Rock. It was here the first explorers found a resting-place, and here was the nucleus for the first settlement in the Mississippi valley.

CHAPTER II.

FATHER MARQUETTE.

A few years ago, while passing through the Vatican at Rome, my attention was called to a department entitled, "Portraits of North American Jesuits." On entering this department, I noticed a life-sized portrait of a man in the garb of a priest, with an open bible in his hands, and a gold cross on his breast. The portrait represented a man in the prime of life, tall and well proportioned, with handsome molded features, and a countenance beaming with intelligence. At the foot of the picture was a motto in Latin, and below it, painted in large Roman letters, was the name of Father Jacques Marquette, a Jesuit priest of North America.

Marquette was born at Leon, in the north part of France, of a wealthy and distinguished family. He was of fine personal appearance, a strong intellect, well educated, and while young became a magnate in his native city. When at a proper age he was ordained a priest, and being enthusiastic about the conversion of heathen, he sailed for America, forsaking home, wealth and friends, to spend a life among the savages in the western world.

After remaining a short time at Quebec, Marquette went west to Lake Huron, where he spent a number of years among the Indians, instructing them in the ways of Christianity. While among the Indians he learned their language, and it is said that he understood and could speak six different Indian dialects.

Marquette went to Sault de Sainte Marie, the outlet of Lake Superior, where Father Allonez had previously established a mission. For a number of years this devout missionary traveled through the lake country, visiting different Indian villages, preaching to the natives, and wherever he went he made many converts to Christianity. Under his preaching old and young came forward to join the church; sometimes baptizing one hundred or more in a day. His active spirit could not rest, causing him to travel from place to place, exposed to inclement weather, wading through water and snow, spending days without shelter or fire, subsisting on parched corn or moss, gathered from rocks. Sometimes paddling his canoe up and down stream, or along the lake shore, and sleeping at night in the open air.

Said Marquette in a letter to a friend in France, " A life in the wilderness has its charms, and the rude hut of a savage is better adapted to a true disciple of Christ, than the palace of a king. My heart oftimes swells with rapture as my canoe glides through strange waters, or while plodding my way through thick forests, among briars and thorns, in laboring for the cause of my Redeemer."

Marquette founded a mission at Mackinaw, and the Indians of different villages along the lake came thither for religious instruction. He built here, on the bank of the lake a small chapel dedicated to St. Ignace, and a few years afterwards he was buried beneath its floor.

DISCOVERY OF THE MISSISSIPPI RIVER.

For many years Indians from the far west, on visiting the French trading post in Canada, spoke of a great river that flowed into the the ocean ; but of the course of this river, and what ocean it emptied into, could not be learned. However, it was believed to empty into the Pacific ocean ; and through it a water communication could be obtained across the continent. The Governor of Canada, knowing the great advantage to be derived from this outlet to the west, selected Louis Joliet, a Canadian by birth, to make the necessary discovery.

Early in the spring of 1673, Joliet was furnished with the necessary outfit for the voyage, and was soon prepared to embark on his hazardous enterprise. Father Marquette, who had acquired much fame among the Indians, on the shore of Lake Huron, was selected to accompany this expedition.

Father Marquette was a devout votary of the Virgin Mary, and to do her bidding he was willing to make any sacrifice. His bold nature knew no fear, and he was prepared to suffer all privations, endure all hardships, in discovering new lands and conquering new realms, to the honor and glory of her Holiness.

Before starting on the tour of discovery, Marquette wrote to a friend in Quebec, saying: "In making this voyage I place myself under the protection of the Holy Virgin, and if she grants me the privilege of seeing the great river of the west, which flows into the Pacific ocean, I will name it in honor of her, "The Immaculate Conception."

All things being ready, Joliet and Marquette, accompained by five companions in two bark canoes, started on their journey. They carried with them a supply of smoked meat and Indian corn, besides a great variety of trinkets for Indian presents.

After a tempestuous voyage, in coasting along the lake shore, they arrived at Green Bay, early in May. Here, at an Indian village they rested for a few days, and during their stay, Marquette preached many times to the natives, exhibiting the picture of the Virgin, Infant Christ, crucifixion, etc., all of which he explained to them. On the morning of the third day after their arrival, Marquette was delighted to see a cross raised in the midst of the village. On this cross were placed deer and buffalo skins, bows and arrows, war-clubs, knives, tomahawks, and scalps taken from the enemy. This cross, said the head chief, was erected in honor of the great French Manito, and all the warriors are commanded to bow down and worship it. On seeing these manifestations of Christianity, Marquette raised his hands heavenward, and thanked God that these heathen of the far west had embraced the true religion, and were therefore, saved from perdition.

After giving the Indians many presents, and pronouncing a blessing upon them, Father Marquette and friends, accompanied by an Indian guide, continued their journey westward. While rowing their canoes up the rapid current of Fox river, they reached a village on its banks, whose inhabitants advised them to go no further on their journey, or their lives would be sacrificed. They told the voyageurs, that the banks of the great river were inhabited by ferocious tribes, who put all strangers to death. That the river was full of frightful monsters, some of which were large enough to swallow a canoe with all its contents. They also said that in a high cliff of rocks by the river side, lived a demon whose roar was so loud as to shake the earth, and destroy all canoes passing up or down the stream; that the stream was full of cataracts and whirlpools, which would engulf them in its foam. These wonderful stories did not frighten the travelers. So after giving the Indians a few presents, and putting their trust in the powers above, continued on their way. Passing up Fox river, and dragging their canoes across the portage, they floated down the Wisconsin. After journeying many days, the river bluffs on each side disappeared, opening up to their view a large plain, while ahead of them was observed a high range of wooded hills. While viewing the wild scene around them, their canoes entered the broad Mississippi, and they found themselves upon the Father of Waters.

The voyageurs landed from their canoes, raised a cross on the bank of the river, and sang praises to the Holy Virgin for her guidance and protection thus far on their journey. Father Marquette pronounced a blessing on the river, and christened it with the most sacred name of "Immaculate Conception." After spending one day in fasting and prayer, their canoes were again put on the water, and they commenced descending the river.

As they were floating down the stream, they discovered on the east bank, near where the city of Alton now stands, a high cliff of rocks rising from the river edge in bold relief, while its image was reflected from the clear waters of the Mississippi. This cliff, for many years afterward, was known as the "Ruined Castle," and is the site of a thrilling legend in Indian tradition. On landing here, they beheld a sight which reminded them that the devil was lord of the wilderness. On the surface of the rock, next to the water, was painted in red, black and green, a pair of monsters, each of which was as large as an ox, with horns like an elk, heads like a tiger, and with frightful expression of countenance. The face of these monsters resembled that of a man— the body covered with scales like a fish—and with tails so long that they reached three times around the body. These terrible looking monsters (representing Indian gods), so frightened Father Marquette that he fled from the place in terror, and hastened on board of his canoe.

As the travelers were passing down the river, conversing about the hideous painting on the rock, they were suddenly aroused to real danger. Here a torrent of dark muddy water came rushing across the clear current of the Mississippi, boiling and surging, sweeping in its course logs, brush and uprooted trees. Their light bark canoes were whirled about on the dark angry water like a small twig in a swollen brook, and with great difficulty their small crafts were kept from swamping in the foaming billows. They had passed the mouth of the Missouri river, and with great rapidity their canoes floated down the rapid stream.

The travelers descended the Mississippi about one thousand miles, to its junction with the Arkansas, when they turned their canoes up stream, and returned to Canada, as has been previously stated.

CHAPTER III.

ILLINOIS INDIANS.

The Illinois Indians were of the Algonquin family, and consisted of five distinct bands, named as follows : Kaskaskias, Cahohias, Peorias, Tamaroas, and Mickgamies. The three former tribes occupied the villages bearing their respective names, and the two latter the country north of Peoria Lake.

According to the statements of early French explorers, these Indians were the most numerous of all the tribes of the west, occupying the country from Lake Michigan to the Mississippi river, and from Rock river to the mouth of the Ohio, being almost the entire territory now included within the State of Illinois. Over this vast country herds of buffalo roamed for their benefit, and the many rivers were navigated by their bark canoes only. From the numerous groves the smoke from their camp fires was seen to ascend, and the lonely forest re-echoed the report of their rifles, as well as their wild war whoops.

They had many towns along the Illinois river, the largest and principal one was La Vantum, which was located near the present site of Utica, an account of which will be given hereafter.

On account of the great abundance of game (it being known far and near as the buffalo country), neighboring tribes frequently made this their hunting grounds, and although the Illinois Indians were not a warlike people, still they would resent an encroachment upon their rights, consequently they were often at war with other tribes.

The Iroquois from the east made frequent raids on the Illinois Indians, destroying their towns, killing squaws and pappooses, and carrying away large quantities of pelts and furs, which they sold to French and English traders.

According to tradition, the Iroquois, in one of these raids, carried off eight hundred prisoners, principally squaws and pappooses, and burned them at their village on the bank of Seneca Lake. The Iroquois Indians having been in trade with the Dutch at Albany, and the French in Canada, had armed themselves with guns, which gave them great advantage over the Illinois, who used bows and arrows only. These war parties of the

Iroquois created so much terror among the Illinois, that they would flee at their approach without offering to give them battle. On account of these frequent raids, the Illinois were much reduced in numbers, which caused them to fall an easy prey to the neighboring tribes some years afterwards.

A little over a century ago, a number of tribes combined, forming an alliance against the Illinois, which resulted in their annihilation, and the occupation of their country by their enemies, as will be shown in the sequel.

LA VANTUM, OR GREAT ILLINOIS TOWN.

The name of La Vantum was applied to the great town of Illinois Indians, more than a century ago, by the French and half-breeds at Peoria. The origin of the name is not known, but is said to be a combination of a French and Indian word, and means a great place, a large town, capital of the tribe, &c. In letters written by Jesuits and early explorers, it is spoken of as the great town of the west, and the chiefs of other villages met here for council. Joliet called this place Kaskaskia, but by La Salle and subsequent explorers, it was known as the great Illinois town. According to the statements of early explorers, this was the

largest town in the western country, being the
headquarters of the Illinois Indians, and the seat
of their trade. The number of its inhabitants
have been variously estimated, ranging from five
to eight thousand. Marquette says he found
here five hundred chiefs and old warriors, and
fifteen hundred braves or young warriors. Seven
years afterward Father Hennepin counted four
hundred and sixty-eight lodges, and these contained from two to four families each. Other accounts are given of it as being a large town,
occupying the river bank for more than a mile,
and extending back some distance on the prairie.

This great Indian town of the west has long
since disappeared, and like many of the ruined
cities of the old world, history and tradition alike
fail to point out its exact location. Some have
located it a little below Buffalo Rock, and others
near the mouth of Little Vermillion, as many Indian relics are found at both of these places. But
in comparing the different accounts given of this
town, from its first discovery by Joliet to the
time of its final destruction, a period of near one
hundred years, it is shown conclusively to have
stood on or near the present site of old Utica.
History says it was on the north bank of the river,
in plain view of Fort St. Louis, and the French
passed to and from it in their canoes.

On the north side of the river is a large bottom prairie, about nine miles in length and one in breadth, extending from the river to the bluff, and from the mouth of Little Vermillion to Buffalo Rock. Near the middle of this prairie, and a few hundred yards below the rapids, the river is confined into a deep, narrow channel. Here the bank rises gradually from the water's edge until it reaches the high land in the rear, forming a sloping plateau, which is elevated above the floods of the Illinois, and for beauty of location is scarcely surpassed by any place on the river.

Forty years ago this point was considered the head of navigation, and consequently the terminus of the Illinois and Michigan canal. In 1834 a town was laid off here by Simon Crozier, and everybody prophesied that it was destined to be a large city. Steamboats at St. Louis put out their sign for Utica, and travelers for the lake country and eastward bound, would land here, and thence proceed by stage to Chicago. Corn is now raised on this town site, two or three old dilapidated buildings only remain of this once great paper city, and Utica, like its predecessor, La Vantum, exists only in history.

Felix La Pance, a French trader at Peoria, frequently visited this town, it being on his route to and from Canada. And he traded with these

Indians from 1751 to 1768, taking their furs with him on his annual trip to Canada, and paying for them in goods on his return. Some account of this town is found among his papers in the possession of his descendants, who are now living on the American Bottom. This account says the town contained from five to six hundred lodges, standing along the river bank for more than a mile in extent. Back on the prairie were a large number of wigwams, or camping tents, occupied part of the year by people from the neighboring villages, who came here each year to raise corn. The town contained from five to eight thousand inhabitants, but at the time of holding their annual feast, nearly all the Illinois nations collected here. On the river bank, about the middle of the town, stood their great council-house, surrounded by stockades and various kinds of fortifications.

The town was shaded by a few out-spreading oaks, in the midst of which, and close to the river bank, was a large spring of cold water. No trees are here at the present time, but there might have been in former days, and killed by fire on the prairie after the town was abandoned. The spring spoken of by La Pance cannot be found on the old town site, but whoever will take the trouble to examine the river at this point when it is low, will observe a short distance from shore the bub-

bles from a spring under water.   Waba, an Indian
chief, who was raised in a village near the mouth
of Fox river, said to one of the fur traders, while
speaking of this town : In his boyhood days there
was here by the side of the trail a large spring of
cold water, and Indians in passing back and forth
would stop here to drink, but afterwards it disappeared and came out under the river.

A short distance from the river, and back of the
old town site, is a range of gravelly knolls, where
the Indians had their caches or subterranean store-
houses, for depositing corn.   The remains of
these caches were plain to be seen in the early
settlement of the country, and in a few instances
these relics still exist.   On the bottom prairie,
above and below the town, for miles in extent, lay
their corn-fields, and east of these was their race-
course, which could be traced out in the early
settlement of the country.   Forty years ago this
prairie showed unmistakable signs of having been
cultivated.   Weeds were found growing here,
which botanists say are never found on the prairie,
except where the sod has been broken*

*It is said that the indians from the neighboring villages came
here during the summer to raise corn, as the land was thought
to produce better crops than elsewhere. The French occupied
this place for thirty-six years, and many of them lived in the
town with the Indians, and were more or less engaged in agricultural pursuits, which may account for the large amount of
land under cultivation.

The high land above and below the town site appears to have been used as a burying ground, on which many skeletons have been exhumed, and various kinds of relics found. James Clark, who owns a large farm here, says every year small pieces of human bones, teeth, beads, arrow heads, &c., as well as implements of Indian and European manufacture, are plowed up. Here in this burying ground, in all probability, many thousand human beings found a long resting place, and the bones of posterity mingled with those of their ancestors. And here are still to be seen a number of artificial mounds, supposed to have been erected over the remains of chiefs or great warriors of past ages. About sixty years ago Waba, a noted Indian chief, opened two of these mounds, from which he took a number of valuable trinkets, consisting of gold and silver medals, crosses, crucifixes, &c. Among the trinkets found here was a silver medallion head of Louis XIV, bearing date 1670, three years before Marquette visited this place, and in all probability it was given to a convert by that holy father.

Here at this great town a large portion of the Illinois Indians would collect during the summer for the purpose of fishing and raising corn, and here were held their annual religious feasts and war dances. During the winter months the Indians would leave their town for Lake Weno, situated about one day's journey westward, for the purpose of collecting furs, and return to their village in early spring.*

*According to Indian tradition, there was a lake about nine leagues west of the great bend in the Illinois river, where the Indians went each winter to collect furs. The Indians called it Lake Weno, (a place of much game), and many allusions are made to it by the first French fur traders.

No such lake now exists, but it is quite probable that there was one in former times, along the valley of Green river, as many things are found here to make this theory plausible· There is a place in Henry county which shows marks of having been a natural dam or obstruction of the river, causing the valley above to be inundated Many things indicate that a large portion of Green river valley was once covered with water, forming a lake thirty miles or more in length, and from one to three in width. The boundaries of this lake are now plain to be seen, by peculiar stratas of earth, which geologists assert are never found except where water once stood. On both sides of the river, along sloughs and small streams, are seen the remains of beaver dams, which are so common on the margin of western lakes.

When the government surveys were made along the valley of Green river, in the year 1821, those having charge of it returned in their notes and so platted many lakes where section corners could not be made, and in maps drawn at that time is shown almost a complete sheet of water. Many places along this valley, which were covered with water in the early settlement of the country, are now only marsh land, subject to occasional overflow, and in time will be brought under cultivation. The obstruction in the river below having worn down by time, and the valley filling up by washings, would cause the lake to disappear and leave it as now seen.

Weno Lake is said to have abounded with beaver, otter and muskrat; the two latter were plenty here in the early settlement of the country, but the former had disappeared.

CHAPTER IV.

THE CROSS RAISED ON THE BANK OF CHICAGO RIVER.

Father Marquette remained at Green Bay but a short time, his health being bad, and the Winnebago Indians with whom he sojourned were unwilling to abandon the religion of their fathers for that of Christianity. It being impressed on the mind of Marquette that his stay on earth would be short, and before departing hence he felt it his duty to again visit the Illinois Indians, and among them establish a mission in honor of the Holy Virgin.

Late in November Marquette left Green Bay, accompanied by two of his countrymen, Pierre and Jacques, together with two Winnebago Indians. The weather was cold, the winds high, and it was with great difficulty they coasted along the western shore of Lake Michigan. Frequently the travelers would be compelled to land from the turbulent water, draw their canoe on the beach, and wait for the winds and waves to subside.

After a long perilous voyage on Lake Michigan, the travelers reached the mouth of Chicago river, and ascended it about three leagues to a grove of timber above the present site of Bridgeport. Here Marquette was taken very sick, so the party could go no further on their way until he recovered. Winter now set in, the river froze up, and the prairie and groves were covered with snow and ice. Near the river bank the companions of Marquette built a hut, covering and siding it with buffalo skins, and here they lived about three months.

Buffalo and deer were plenty, and the Indians from a neighboring village supplied them with corn, honey and maple sugar, so they did not lack for the necessaries of life. For many days Marquette was prostrated by disease so he could not rise from his couch, and his friends believed that his time of departure was nigh. Having a great desire to establish a mission among the Indians before he died, he begged his two companions— Pierre and Jacques—to join him in nine days' devotion to the Virgin, and through her interposition his disease relented, and he gained strength daily.

Indians from a village two leagues distant,

frequently visited their hut, and Marquette, feeble
as he was, preached to them, and by the power of
his eloquence many became Christians. Near
their hut they built of cottonwood poles a temporary altar, and over which was raised a large
wooden cross. The converted Indians were
taught to look upon this cross while praying, and
thereby all their sins were remitted. Many mir-
acles are said to have been wrought among the
Indians by looking upon this sacred talisman—
the blind were made to see and the sick restored
to health. For many days the Indians continued
to worship at the altar, Father Marquette
preaching and laying his hands on their
heads, would bestow his blessing on them. A
beloved chief, who for years had been afflicted
with a demon in his back, so he could not raise
from his couch, was carried to Marquette, and
when the holy father laid his hands upon him, in
the name of the Virgin, the demon departed and
the chief was restored to health.

In March the country was flooded with water,
and Marquette's health being partially restored,
they put their canoe on the river and contiuued
their journey westward. Although Marquette
was gone, his magic power over the Indians remained. They hallowed the spot where the altar
stood, and when the rude structure rotted down,

they erected an earthen mound on its site, so the
spot should not be forgotten by coming genera-
tions.   Although two centuries have passed away,
this mound is still to be seen, and among the
French and Indians there are many remarkable
traditions in relation to it.   The Indians from
different villages, according to tradition, were in
the habit of collecting here once a year—on the
fifth day of the tenth moon—and offer up prayers
and sacrifices to the Great Manito of the French,
in order that they might be successful in war,
fishing, hunting, &c.

About fifty years after Marquette had raised
the cross here, Charlevoix, with a party of French
explorers, visited this country, and while rowing
their canoes up the Chicago river they found collected on this spot a large body of Indians,
engaged in devotional exercises.   On the mound
stood a wooden cross, partly covered with a bear
skin, and around it the Indians were kneeling in
prayer.   Charlevoix and friends landed from
their canoes, and spent the day worshiping with
the Indians, and to them Father Canabe, a Jesuit
priest, administered the sacrament.*

*In the early settlement of Chicago, this place was known to
many of the French Catholics, some of whom visited it in
memory of its sainted founder—Father Marquette. This place
was the scene of another remarkable incident, which will appear in another part of this book.

MISSION OF IMMACULATE CONCEPTION.

The winter was now over, snow and ice had disappeared from the prairies, and the warm sun of early spring not only animated nature, but it gave strength and vitality to Father Marquette. His cough had almost ceased; his tall, manly form, which had been bent by rheumatism, was now erect, and he sang songs of praise to the Holy Virgin for his restoration to health. After taking an affectionate farewell of the Indians, Marquette, with his two companions, left in their bark canoe for the great Illinois town.

With sail and oars the voyageurs urged their canoe down the Illinois river, while the surrounding woods re-echoed their songs of praise. Birds were singing among the branches of trees, squirrels chirping in the groves, while elk and deer bounded away at the sound of the approaching canoe. Swans, pelicans and wild geese would rise from the water and fly squawking down stream, while beaver and otter were sporting in the river, and diving under their canoe. Far and near the prairie was covered with buffalo, some basking in the sun, while others were feeding on the early spring grass. Morning and evening long lines of buffalo were seen coming to the river to drink, sometimes swimming the stream or climbing the banks and shaking the water from their shaggy sides, while gazing wildly at the passing canoe.

When Marquette arrived at La Vantum, the Indians received him as though he was an angel from heaven, some of whom fell on their knees before him, asking forgiveness for past sins. Chassagoac, the head chief, who Marquette had baptized the year before, was so delighted at meeting the holy father that he embraced him and wept for joy.

On the day following Marquette's arrival, all the Indians, both old and young, assembled on the meadow above the town to hear good tidings from the great French Manito, (the name given to Jesus Christ). Around Marquette were seated on the ground five hundred old chiefs and warriors, and behind them stood fifteen hundred young braves, while back of these were collected all the squaws and pappooses of the town. Marquette, standing in the midst of this vast assembly, displayed to them two pictures painted on canvas, one of the Virgin and the other of Jesus Christ, telling them of God, of heaven, and of hell, when all the Indians clapped their hands and shouted for joy. By direction of Marquette, the Indians tore down the temple and images erected to the god of war, and built a chapel on its site.

This chapel was constructed by setting poles in the ground, siding and covering it with elk and deer skins. Notwithstanding it was very large— capable of holding one thousand or more persons —so many workmen were employed that it was completed on the third day. When the house of God was ready for use, all the chiefs and old warriors assembled therein, when Marquette dedicated it in honor of the Holy Virgin, giving it the same name that he had already given to the Mississippi river—" The Immaculate Conception."

Every day the chapel was filled with Indians, and Marquette preached to them, calling on the warriors to forsake the religion of their fathers and embrace Christianity. Many came forward and joined the church, and one hundred or more were baptized at a time. For a number of weeks Marquette preached daily to the Indians, baptizing and instructing them in the ways of Christianity.

On Easter Sunday the chapel was decorated with evergreens, representing crosses, anchors, crucifixes, &c. Incense was burned on the altar, and lights were kept burning during the day, according to the custom of the Catholic church. The woods far and near had been searched for geese and turkey eggs, which were beautifully colored and distributed among the converts, in commemoration of Christ's resurrection.   The day was a joyous one for the Indians, and it was long remembered by them, but with it ended the ministry of Marquette among the red men of the west.

Spring had now come ; the groves were once more green, and the prairie was covered with grass and flowers, but it did not bring health and vigor to the fast-failing priest.   His disease had again returned in its worst form, and he felt that his life was fast passing away.   After spending two days and nights in prayer, communing with Christ and the Holy Virgin, he concluded to return to Canada, where he could receive the sacrament from the hands of his brethren before he died.

On the third week after Easter, the Indians were assembled in the chapel, when Marquette, pale and feeble as he was, instructed them in the ways of Christianity, telling them that he was about to depart for Canada, but promised to send a priest to teach them in the ways of salvation. The Indians heard the news in sadness, gathering around the holy father; and begged him to remain with them.   But he told them that his work was ended—that a few weeks would close his pilgrimage here on earth, and before he departed hence he desired to return to Canada, and there leave his bones among his countrymen.

Marquette's canoe was once more put on the water, and with his two faithful companions he commenced his journey eastward. About five hundred warriors, some in canoes and others mounted on ponies, accompanied Marquette as far as Lake Michigan, and then received from him the parting blessing.

After parting with the Indians, Marquette's canoe started around the head of the lake, and with sail hoisted and oars applied, they coasted along the southern shore with the expectation of reaching Canada in about five weeks. Pierre and Jacques with all their power plied the oars to increase their speed, while the sick priest lay prostrated in the bottom of the canoe, communing with the Virgin and with angels.

DEATH OF MARQUETTE.

When near the mouth of St. Joseph river, Marquette felt that his time had come, and he told his companions to land him on the beach of the lake, in order that he might receive the sacrament before he died. On a high piece of land, at the mouth of a small stream which still bears his name, they built a bark shanty, and carried thither the dying priest. With his eyes fixed on a crucifix, which one of his companions held before him, and while murmuring the name of Mary and Jesus, he breathed his last. His companions dug a grave on the bank of the stream, near the spot where he died, and buried him there. In obedience to his request, they erected a large cross, made of basswood timber, over his grave, on which was engraved his name and date of his death. After burying Marquette, Pierre and Jacques again put their canoe on the lake and continued their journey toward Canada, conveying thither the sad news of his death.

Three years after Marquette's death, a party of Indians of Mackinaw, who had been converted to Christianity some years before under his preaching, went to Lake Michigan, opened the grave, and took up his remains. After washing and drying the bones, they placed them in a box made of birch bark and carried them to Mackinaw. With the remains of the holy father they turned their canoes homeward, singing and chanting praises as they went along. Seven miles above Mackinaw they were met by a large delegation of Indians in canoes, who formed a procession to escort the remains to the mission. With their faces blacked, oars muffled, and singing a funeral dirge, the procession slowly approached the mission, and were met at the landing by priest, traders and Indians, all of whom wore badges of mourning. With a solemn ceremony the remains of Father Marquette were received at the mission, and buried beneath the little chapel of St. Ignace, which he had built some years before. On the following day Father Allonez preached to the Indians collected here, and a large number of them embraced Christianity and were baptized.

Two centuries have now passed away since the burial of Marquette, and long since the little chapel of St. Ignace has gone to decay, but the spot where it stood was hallowed by the French and converted Indians, and is now pointed out to strangers.

For many years after the death of Marquette, the French sailors on the lakes kept his picture nailed to the mast-head as a guardian angel, and when overtaken by a storm they would pray to the holy father, beseeching him to calm the wind and still the troubled waters, in order that they might reach port in safety.

CHAPTER V.

Seven years after Joliet and Marquette discovered the upper Mississippi, La Salle obtained a patent from the king of France, authorizing him to explore and take possession of all the country west of the great lakes. La Salle's success and failures in this enterprise is a matter of history, and foreign to our purpose, but as his name appears in connection with many incidents, a few facts relating to him may be of interest to the reader.

Robert Cavalier (La Salle being a title only) was born in the year 1643, in the city of Rouen, of wealthy parentage, and was educated for the priesthood. In person he is said to have been large and muscular, possessing a fine intellect, an iron constitution, and well qualified for the enterprise in which he embarked. He inherited from his ancestors a large fortune, which was used in advancing his enterprise, but was squandered in

consequence of misplaced confidence in those
with whom he associated. Although La Salle
made his mark in history, his life was one of
hardships, exposure and deprivations, and he
finally died by the hand of an assassin in the
wilds of Texas.

A few years ago, while strolling through the
city of Rouen, my guide pointed out an old
palace standing on high ground, and overlooking
the river Seine. For beauty of architecture and
antique appearance, this palace has no equal in
the old Norman capital. This old palace, said
my guide, was once the residence of the duke of
Normandy, afterwards known as William the
Conqueror, and from its portico this great warrior
addressed his lords and nobles on the day he left
Normandy for the conquest of England. In this
palace, continued my guide, now lives Count
Cavalier, a descendant of the family of La Salle.
Two squares distant from here is an antique looking house, pointed out as the birth place, and for
some time the residence of the great explorer,
La Salle, and is still occupied by his family de-
scendants.

LA SALLE AND PARTY WESTWARD BOUND.

In the summer of 1669, La Salle built a vessel
on Niagara river, above the falls, for the purpose

of navigating the upper lakes. This vessel was of sixty tons burden, carrying lateen-sails, and named the Griffin. It was armed with a number of small cannon, and a large wooden eagle surmounted its prow. On the day of departure the vessel was visited by a large body of Indians, who were astonished at this great canoe, as they called it, as nothing like it had ever been seen on the upper lakes before. Father Hennepin preached to these Indians from the deck of the Griffin, when they clapped their hands, shouting and yelling in response to his words, and offered him presents to be used as sacrifices to the great Manito of the French*

All things being ready, the cannons fired a salute, the sails were spread to the breeze, and the Griffin moved forward, plowing through the maiden waves of Lake Erie†

---

*An ingenious Frenchman painted on canvas a colossal picture of a griffin, according to Grecian mythology. This monster had the body of a lion, with the wings of an eagle, representing strength and swiftness. This picture (the motto of the vessel) was stretched between the masts, and the Indians mistook it for the French Manito or god, so they bowed down and worshiped it.

†In La Salle's party was an Italian officer, second in command, named Tonti, who figures extensively in our narrative, and a short account of whom will be found elsewhere. In this party were also three Jesuit priests, Louis Hennepin, Gabriel Rebourde, and Zenobe Membre. The former of these priests is known in history by his surname, and the two latter by their given names.

After a number of days sail, the vessel passed
through a small lake, which La Salle gave the
name of St. Clair, in honor of that saint whose
name appeared that day in the calendar.   On the
following day, after passing Lake St. Clair, they
were overtaken by a terrible storm, which threatened the vessel with destruction, and all on board
believed their time had come.   The rolling of
the vessel and lashing of the waves, caused
the sailors to hold fast to the bulwarks to prevent being carried overboard.   Father Hennepin
in his journal says that he joined with others in
fervent prayer to St. Anthony, making a solemn
vow to that saint if he would deliver them from
their peril with which they were surrounded, the
first chapel built in the new discovered country
should be dedicated to him.   The saint heard
their prayers—the wind calmed, and the Griffin
continued on her way, while plunging through the
foaming billows.

After a voyage of four weeks, the Griffin arrived at Mackinaw, and was safely moored in the
harbor of St. Ignace.   Here at the straits of Mackinaw was an Indian village, a Jesuit mission, and
the seat of a large fur trade.   Both French and
Indians collected around the vessel in great astonishment, as nothing larger than a bark canoe
was ever seen there before.   The goods brought

by the Griffin were exchanged for furs at a large profit, and the vessel, loaded with pelts, started back for Niagara, but was never heard of afterwards.*

Late in November La Salle, accompanied by fourteen persons, left Mackinaw in four canoes, and coasted along the shore of Lake Michigan in a southern direction. They carried with them a blacksmith's forge, carpenter tools, and other utensils required in building a fort, besides a large amount of merchandise to trade with the Indians.

On the second day out, they were overtaken by a storm, which compelled them to land, drag their canoes on the beach, and there remain four days for the angry waters to subside. Again trusting their frail barks to the waters of Lake Michigan, they found themselves on the following day overtaken by a severe gale, and amid the lashing of waves their canoes drifted on a barren, rocky island, some distance from the main land. Here on this rocky island they remained two days and nights, without shelter or fire, and their blankets alone protected them from the cold winter blast.

---

*The fate of the Griffin was never known. Some thought she perished in a gale, others that she was burned by the Indians, and the crew put to death. But La Salle believed that the crew, after disposing of the furs and pelts for their own benefit, burned the vessel and fled the country to escape punishment.

When the wind and waves subsided, they again continued their journey, but a new trouble overtook them. Having been so long on the water, their stock of provisions became exhausted, and three of the party went in search of an Indian village, in order to obtain a supply. On the following day a large party of Indians came to their camp, bringing with them corn and venison, which they exchanged for goods. These Indians encamped near the French, and during the night amused them with songs and dances.

It was cold weather when the travelers reached the mouth of St. Joseph river, and here they remained for a few days waiting for Tonti and his companions. On the arrival of Tonti the party, consisting of thirty-five persons in bark canoes, commenced ascending St. Joseph river.*

*History says the Griffin went to Green Bay, and from there La Salle and companions started in their canoes for Illinois. But this is not probable, as there was no trading post at Green Bay at that time, and it was not likely that the vessel would go any further west than trade had gone. If the voyageurs had landed at Green Bay, they would have followed along the western shore of Lake Michigan to the mouth of Chicago river, ascending that stream, and down the Des Plaines to Illinois. This route was known at the time to the French, as Joliet and Marquette passed over it seven years before. La Salle and party could not have crossed Lake Michigan in their canoes, and it is highly improbable that they followed around its southern end, as it would be out of their course.

Two years before this expedition, Father Allonez established a mission at the mouth of St. Joseph's river, and at this point

On arriving at or near the present site of South
Bend, they stopped to search for the path which
led across the portage to the head waters of Kankakee. While thus engaged, La Salle lost his
reckoning, and in the thick forest he rambled
about all day and a part of the night, during a
severe snow storm. Many times he fired his gun
as a signal to his friends, but received from them
no response. About two o'clock in the morning
he discovered through the thick undergrowth a
gleam of light, and he hastened thither, supposing
it to be his camp, but was disappointed at finding
no one there. By the side of the fire was a bed
made of dry grass and leaves, which was still
warm, the occupant having been frightened away
at his approach. La Salle called out in different
Indian dialects, but received no reply, so he laid
down on the deserted bed and slept until morning. The former occupant of this bed was never
known, but supposed to have been an Indian
hunter.

they expected to meet Tonti with twenty men, who came from
Mackinaw by land. It is said Tonti and his party got lost among
thick forests and lakes of Michigan, and did not reach their
destination for some time after La Salle's arrival.

There is an old traditionary acount of this affair, which says
La Salle and party were afraid to trust their frail barks again
on the angry waters of the lake in mid winter, after their past
experience, and therefore went by the way of St. Joseph and
Kankakee rivers.

The friends of La Salle were very much alarmed
at his long absence, and during the night they
fired guns and beat their drum in order to direct
him to camp, but without effect.   They had about
given him up as lost, when about four o'clock on
the following day they saw him approaching the
camp with two opossums hanging from his belt.*

The canoes were carried across the portage, five
miles in width, put on the water of the Kankakee, and floated down that stream and the Illinois
river to La Vantum, the great town of Illinois.
It was now mid winter, and they found the town
deserted, its occupants having gone off on their
winter hunt, in accordance with their custom.
Being in a starving condition, La Salle ordered
one of the caches opened, and took therefrom
twenty minots of corn, hoping at some future
time to compensate the Indians for this robbery.
After spending two days in the desolate lodges
of the town, the party again boarded their canoes
and continued on their way down the river.

About five leagues below La Vantum, at the
mouth of a stream—supposed to have been Bureau
creek—the voyageurs landed and sent out a party
to hunt buffalo.   The hunters were successful in
their search, and on coming up with a large herd

---

* "Parkman's Discovery of the Great West."

of buffalo, a short distance from the river; they killed two of them and returned to camp with the meat. This supply of meat, with the corn they took from the Indian store-house, drove hunger from their camp, and the three priests joined in returning thanks to the Holy Virgin for thus providing for their wants, while journeying through this wild wilderness country.

The following day being New Year, 1680, it was agreed to spend it in camp worshiping, saying mass, and taking sacrament in accordance to an old custom in the Catholic Church.

Before leaving Canada, Father Hennepin provided himself with a miniature altar, which folded up like an army chair, and could be carried on the back the same as a knapsack. With this altar on his back, Father Hennepin started off through the woods in search of a suitable place for worship, followed by the other priests and the rest of the party. A place was selected, the altar erected, and the holy father preached to his companions, causing the woods to resound with his loud exhortations and songs of praise. After preaching and saying mass, the sacred emblems were placed by the side of the altar, preparatory to taking the sacrament. But great was Father Hennepin's surprise to find the wine vessel empty, as one of the party, a blacksmith by trade, and nicknamed

La Forge, had drank it up while on the road.
For this act of sacrilege, Father Hennepin pronounced against him a curse, equal to the one
Pope Leo pronounced against Martin Luther for
publishing the Bible.

THE FRENCH AT PEORIA LAKE.

According to history, on the 3d of January,
1680, the inhabitants of an Indian village situated
on the west bank of Peoria Lake, were much
surprised to see eight canoes filled with armed
men opposite their town.   The canoes were all
abreast, presenting a formidable appearance, and
the men seated in them held guns in their hands,
ready for an attack or defence.   These canoes
rounded to and landed at the village, causing a
great panic among the Indians, some of whom
fled in terror, while others seized their arms and
prepared to defend themselves.   Amid the confusion that followed, La Salle sprang ashore, and
presented to the astonished Indians the calumet,
(a token of friendship), while Father Hennepin
caught several frightened children and soothed
their fears with kindness and small presents.

The French pitched their tent in the Indian
village, and remained for some days.   But dis-

contentment among the men, and fearing treachery of the Indians, caused La Salle to remove to a place of greater security. A site was selected, a fort built, and all the valuables at their camp transferred thereto. On account of the gloomy prospects, the discontentment and desertion of some of the men, La Salle named this fort Creve Ceour, which in the French language means broken heart.*

Fort Creve Ceour consisted of stockades, enclosing a small plat of ground, and within which were a number of log cabins—quarters for officers and soldiers. Father Hennepin lamented the loss of wine, which prevented him from administering the sacrament, but each morning and evening all the occupants of the fort were summoned to his cabin for prayer. Father Gabriel and Zenobe spent most of their time in the Indian village, preaching to and instructing the natives in the ways of Christianity, but they made but few proselytes.

About the first of February Father Hennepin, in a canoe, accompanied by two companions, left the fort on a voyage of discovery. Passing down

*The exact location of this fort is not known, but it is believed to have stood on the east side of the river, about three miles below the outlet of the lake, at a place now called Wesley. This place answers the description given by Hennepin, and also accords with traditionary accounts.

to the mouth of the Illinois river, they ascended
the Mississippi as far as the falls of St. Anthony.
Here Hennepin was made a prisoner by the Indians, and remained with them some months, but
was finally set at liberty, reached Canada in safety,
returned to France and published a book of his
travels.

Early in the spring La Salle returned to Canada to procure men and supplies, leaving Tonti
in command of the fort.   A short time after La
Salle's departure, all the soldiers except three
deserted their post, ascending the river in canoes,
and coasting around the shore of Lake Michigan
they reached Mackinaw in safety.   Tonti, being
left with the two priests and three soldiers, abandoned the fort, and it was never occupied
afterwards.

CHAPTER VI.

HENRI DE TONTI.

Among the many adventurers who accompanied
La Salle to America and took part in exploring
the wilds of the west, was an Italian of noble
birth by the name of Henri de Tonti. Some
years before, young Tonti, with his father's family,
were banished from Italy, on account of having
taken part in a revolution of that country, and they
found a home in Rouen, France. Tonti, having
a military education, joined the French army, and
served five years, a part of the time as captain, in
the National Guards. At the close of the war
he was discharged from service, came to America
and joined La Salle in his enterprise. La Salle
made Tonti his lieutenant, or second in command,
and the sequel shows that he was worthy of the
trust placed in him.

Tonti's right hand having been shot off in the
Sicilian war, its place was supplied with an iron
one, which he kept always covered with a glove.

With this iron hand, Tonti, on different occasions, broke the heads or knocked out the teeth of disorderly Indians, which caused them to believe that he possessed supernatural power.

Tonti brought with him from France a large sum of money, which he used in common with La Salle in exploring and taking possession of the west, as well as in trade with the Indians.

The late Dr. Sparks says history never can do ample justice to Tonti. His life was one of patriotism and self-sacrifice, and the discovery and taking possession of the great west belong mainly to him.

Forty years of Tonti's life was spent in the wilds of the west, enduring hardships, dangers, and deprivations, associating with savages, and without the benefits and comforts of civilization. His fortune sacrificed—his health and manhood destroyed—he became a wanderer along the gulf of Mexico, but at last returned to die at Fort St. Louis, and his bones now rest on the bank of the Illinois river, at the west end of Starved Rock.

In one of the Louvre picture galleries in Paris, can be seen a full-length portrait of a youthful looking man, dressed in French uniform, with epaulets on his shoulders and an eagle on his breast. His left hand holds a sword, while the left presents a singular appearance, as though deformed, but is hidden by a glove. This tall, graceful figure, and the piercing black eyes, never fails to attract the attention of strangers, and inquiry would naturally arise for the history of the person here represented. Below this portrait is painted in large letters the name—" *Henri de Tonti, la voyageur des Amerique.*"

THE FRENCH AT LA VANTUM.

After most of the soldiers had deserted from Fort Creve Ceour, Tonti, with those remaining, consisting of Father Gabriel, Father Zenobe and three soldiers, abandoned the place. All the valuables in the fort were put into two canoes, and the party ascended the river as far as La Vantum. Here they found quarters among the Indians, with the intention of awaiting La Salle's return from Canada. Tonti applied himself in learning the Indian language—the two priests were engaged in preaching to the natives—while the soldiers were spending the honeymoon with their squaws, whom they had recently married.

About three miles from the town, in the midst of a thick grove of timber, Father Gabriel and Zenobe erected a temporary altar, and every third day they repaired thither for prayer and meditation. Here in this lonely spot, far away from the noise and bustle of the town, the two holy Friars would spend long summer days, from early morning until late at night, communing with the Virgin, saints and angels.

Notwithstanding these priests preached and prayed with these Indians almost daily, promising them success in war, hunting, &c., if they would embrace Christianity, but few converts were made. Chassagoac, the head chief, having embraced the Christian religion seven years before, under the preaching of Father Marquette, still continued in the faith.   The chief, his household, and a few of his friends, had taken the sacrament from the hands of the priests, but all the other chiefs and principal warriors denounced Christianity, adhering to the religion of their fathers.

The wine brought from Canada for sacramental purposes having been drank by La Forge, as previously stated, it became necessary to procure a substitute, as the administration of the sacred rights could not be dispensed with.   During the winter the priests gathered a quantity of wild grapes, pressed out the juice and put it away in the sacramental cask for future use.   This wine answered the purpose very well so long as the weather remained cool, but during the summer it soured and became unfit for use.

The time came to administer the sacrament.

Tonti, the three soldiers with their wives, Chassagoac and family, with a few friends, were assembled in the council-house on the Sabbath day to receive the sacred emblems. Father Gabriel, wrapped in his long black robe, with a gold cross suspended from his neck, preached to them, speaking of Christ, of the apostles, of saints, and of the kingdom to come. After preaching, all knelt around the altar engaged in prayer, while Father Gabriel made preparations to administer the sacrament; but he was horrified to find the wine sour, and the miracle of transubstantiation (that is, converting it into the real blood of Christ) could not be performed, consequently the sacramental service was postponed until another day.

Time hung heavy with the French; days and weeks passed away; spring was gone, the summer almost ended, and no news from La Salle. In an Indian village, where there is neither hunting or war parties, nor national dances to keep up the excitement, it has a dull, monotonous appearance. Warriors lay under the shade of trees, sleeping or amusing themselves in games of chance, while squaws were at work in cornfields, or preparing food for their families. Naked children were playing on the green or rolling in the dirt, while young maidens, with their lovers, were gathering flowers in the grove, fishing on

the banks of the river, or rowing their canoes
across its waters, unconscious of the great calamity
that was about to befall them.

THE ALARM AND PREPARATION FOR DEFENSE.

It was near the close of a warm day in the
latter part of August, 1680, when a scout arrived
with his horse in a foam of sweat, and shouting at
the top of his voice that the Iroquois were
marching against the town.   All was now excitement and confusion ; squaws screamed, pappooses
quit their plays on the green, and ran away to
their homes; warriors caught their weapons and
made preparations to defend their town and protect their squaws and little ones.   During the
night fires were kept burning along the river
bank, and every preparation made to defend the
town in case it should be attacked.   The warriors
greased their bodies, painted their faces red, and
ornamented their heads with turkey feathers;
war songs were sung, drums beat; warriors
danced, yelled and brandished their war clubs to
keep up their courage.   At last morning came,
and with it the savage Iroquois.

When news came of the approaching Iorquois,
a crowd of excited savages collected around
Tonti and his companions, whom they had previ-

ously suspected of treachery, and charged them
with being in league with their enemies. A
report having reached them that a number of
Jesuit priests, and even La Salle himself was with
the Iroquois, and leading them on to the town.
The enraged warriors seized the blacksmith forge,
tools, and all the goods that belonged to the
French, and threw them into the river. One of
the warriors caught Tonti by the hair of his head
and raised his tomahawk to split his skull, but a
friendly chief caught the savage by the arm, and
his life was spared. Tonti, with that boldness
and self-possession which was characteristic of
him, defended himself against these charges, and
in order to convince them of his good faith,
offered to accompany them to battle.

Father Gabriel and Zenobe were away at their
altar, spending the day in prayer and meditation,
and had no warning of the danger that awaited
them. On their return home late at night, they
were surprised to find the town in a whirlpool of
excitement; squaws were crying and bewailing
their fate, while the warriors were dancing, yelling
and offering up sacrifices to the Manito of battle.

On the arrival of the two priests, the savages
collected around them, charging them with treachery, and being the cause of the Iroquois invading
their country. The priests, with uplifted hands,

called God to witness their innocence of the charge, but their statement did not change the minds of the excited Indians. A loud clamor was raised for their blood, and a number of warriors sprang forward with uplifted tomahawks to put an end to their existence, but as they drew nigh and were about to tomahawk them, Father Gabriel drew from his bosom a small gold image of the Holy Virgin, and held it up before their would-be executioners. On seeing this sacred talisman the Indians paused a moment, and then returned their tomahawks to their belts. Father Zenobe afterwards said this was another proof of the Virgin protecting the Jesuits in North America.

During the night all the squaws and pappooses, with the old Indians unable to bear arms, were placed in canoes and taken down the river about three leagues, to a large marshy island.* About sixty warriors were left for their protection, and all of them secreted themselves in the reeds and high grass, so they could not be seen by the Iroquois. But the sequel shows that they did not escape the vigilance of the enemy, and this island of supposed safety became their tomb.

*This island is situated between the river and Lake Depue, and consits of several hundred acres of marsh land, a part of which is covered during the summer with reeds and bulrushes Formerly it was surrounded by water, but from the washings of the river the upper end is filled up so that in an ordinary stage of water it connects with the main land.

CHAPTER VII.

THE BATTLE AND MASSACRE.

At the time of the Iroquois invasion, there were only about five hundred warriors at La Vantum, the head chief, Chassagoac, and a large portion of his braves having gone to Cahokia for the purpose of attending a religious feast. But this band, small as it was, boldly crossed the river at daylight, and met the enemy, whose number was five times as large as their own. While they were ascending the bluff a scout met them, saying that the enemy were crossing the prairie between the Vermillion and Illinois timber. As the invaders approached the river timber, they were surprised to meet the Illinoians, who were lying in ambush, and received them with a deadly fire. At this unexpected attack, the Iroquois were stricken with a panic and fled from the field, leaving the ground covered with the dead and wounded. But they soon rallied and the fight became bloody, arrows and rifle balls flying thick

and fast, while the woods far and near resounded
with the wild whoops of contending savages.

In the midst of the fight, Tonti undertook the
perilous task of mediating between the contending parties. Laying aside his gun and taking a
wampum belt in his hand, holding it over his
head as a flag of truce, and amid showers of
arrows and bullets, he walked boldly forward to
meet the enemy. As he approached, the Iroquois
warriors collected around him in a threatening
manner, one of whom attempted to stab him to
the heart, but the knife striking a rib inflicted
only a long, shallow gash. As the savage
was about to repeat the blow a chief came
up, and seeing he was a white man, protected
him from further assault, and applied a bandage
to the wound to stop its bleeding. The fighting
having ceased, a warrior took Tonti's hat, and
placing it on the muzzle of his gun, started
toward the Illinoians, who, on seeing it, supposed
he was killed and again renewed the fight.
While the battle was in progress, a warrior
reported that three Frenchmen, armed with guns,
were with the Illinois forces, and firing on them.
When this announcement was made the Iroquois
became enraged at Tonti, and again gathered
around him, some for killing and others for his
protection. One of the warriors caught him by

the hair of his head, raising it up, and with his long knife was about to take off his scalp, when Tonti, with his iron hand, knocked down his assailant Others attacked Tonti with knives and tomahawks, but he was again rescued from death by the head-chief.

For a long time the battle raged, many of the combatants on both sides being slain, and the yells of the warriors could be heard far away. But at last the Illinoians, whose force was inferior to their adversary, were overpowered and driven from the field. The vanquished fled to their town, with the intention of defending it or perish in the attempt.

On the river bank, near the center of the town, was their great council-house, surrounded by stockades, forming a kind of fortification. To this the remnant of the warriors fled, and in great haste tore down the lodges and used the material in strengthening their works.

The Illinoians had crossed the river in canoes, but their pursuers having no means of crossing at this point, were obliged to go up to the rapids where they forded it. In a short time the Iroquois attacked the town, setting fire to the lodges and fortifications, which were soon a mass of flames. Many of the beseiged were burned in their strongholds, others were slain or taken prisoners as they escaped from the flames; a few only succeeded in the preservation of their lives by escaping down the river. The town, with the great council-house and fortifications, was destroyed by fire, and nothing was left of them except the blackened poles of which the lodges were constructed.

When the victory was completed they bound the prisoners hand and foot, and commenced torturing them to make them reveal the hiding place of their squaws and pappooses.

On obtaining the necessary information a large war party took the canoes left by the vanquished Illinoians, and descended the river in search of the squaws and pappooses. While these defenseless beings were secreted among the reeds and high grass of the island, they were discovered by the savage Iroquois, and all of them slain. The sixty warriors left to guard them fled on the approach of the enemy, crossing the lake and secreting themselves in the thick river timber.

TORTURING THE PRISONERS.

On the following day after the battle, the victors made preparations to torture the prisoners; and their acts of barbarity probably never have been equaled by any of the savages of the west. The warriors were formed into a large circle, and the prisoners, bound hand and foot, were conveyed thither, when the work of torture commenced. The doomed prisoners were seated on the ground awaiting their fate, some of whom were weeping or praying, while others were engaged in singing their death song. A warrior, with a long knife, cut off the nose and ears of the prisoners, and threw them to their hungry dogs. Pieces of flesh were cut out of their arms and breasts, while the prisoners sat writhing with agony; and the ground around them red with human gore. The work of torture went on—the executioners continued to cut off limbs and pieces of flesh—and in some cases the bowels were taken out and trailed on the ground, while the groans and screams of the victims in their death agonies were terrible to witness.

Tonti and his companions looked on these barbarous acts of the Iroquois with horror and astonishment, but dare not remonstrate as they were prisoners also, and did not know but a like fate awaited them.

While the torture was going on the two priests were engaged in baptizing the victims, in order to absolve them from past sins, and as each one was about to expire, they would hold the crucifix before his eyes, so he might look on it, and through its divine efficacy his soul would be saved from perdition.

When the prisoners were all dead, the warriors cut out their hearts, roasted and eat them in order to make them brave.

For a number of days the Iroquois continued to rejoice over their victory, spending the time in singing and dancing around the scalps, and causing the timber and river bluffs to re-echo with their yells and wild whoops.

DEATH OF FATHER GABRIEL.

Two days after the Iroquois victory, the French were set at liberty, and they departed in an old leaky canoe. After going about six leagues, they stopped at the mouth of a large creek to repair the canoe and dry their clothing. While thus engaged, Father Gabriel, who was always fond of solitude, wandered off into the thick river timber for the purpose of prayer and meditation. When the canoe was repaired, clothes dried, and time of departure came, Father Gabriel was missing, and they searched for him among the thick timber, but he could not be found. During the night fires were kept burning along the river bank, and guns discharged to direct him to camp, but all in vain.   During the following day they searched the woods far and near for the missing priest, and Father Zenobe prayed to the Holy Virgin for his safe return, but all to no purpose, so they gave him up for lost, and continued their journey.   For many days they mourned the loss of the holy father, as he was an old man of nearly three score years, and devoted to the work of the church.

It was afterwards ascertained that Father Gabriel was taken prisoner by the Indians, carried to their camp some miles off, where he was executed, and while his friends were searching for him those savages were dancing around his scalp.

While Father Gabriel was at prayer in the thick timber, some distance from his companions, he was approached by two Indians in a threatening manner.   With his head uncovered he arose to meet them, with one hand pointing heavenward and the other to the gold cross on his breast, giving them to understand that he was a priest. In vain he told them that he was their friend, and had come from afar across the big waters to teach them in the ways of truth and happinesss.   Regardless of his entreaties, they bound his hands behind his back and led him off a prisoner to their camp.   A council was held over the captives and it was decided that he should die. A stake was driven into the ground, and Father

Gabriel with his hands and feet pinioned, tied to it. Here, he sat on the ground bound to the stake, with his long hair and flowing beard white with the snows of seventy winters, waving to and fro in the wind. The Indians formed a circle around their victim, singing and dancing while flourishing their war-clubs over his head, and occasionally yelling at the top of their voices. This performance continued for some time, while the victim sat with his head bowed down, his eyes fixed on the gold cross which hung on his breast, and in silence awaited his doom.

Under repeated blows of war-clubs, Father Gabriel fell to the ground and soon expired. His clothing and scalp were taken off by the savages, and his remains left to be devoured by wolves.

Thus perished Father Gabriel, the only heir of a wealthy Burgundian house, who had given up a life of ease and comfort, with all the enjoyment of riches and society in the old world, to preach the gospel to the heathens of the west, whom at last became his murderers.

Four years after this affair, a trader at Fort St. Louis bought of an Indian a small gold image of the Virgin Mary, with Father Gabriel's name and that of the owner engraved thereon. This image was presented to Father Gabriel the day he sailed for America, by the cardinal bishop of Normandy, and he carried it in his bosom near his heart until the day of his death. Some years afterward, this golden image was carried back to France, and is now to be seen in the museum at Rouen.

A SCENE OF HORROR.

It was mid winter, three months after the massacre of the Illinois Indians, when La Salle, with twelve companions, returned from Canada to look after his little colony on the Illinois river. As the travelers urged their canoes down the swollen stream, their eyes were directed to Starved Rock, where they expected to find Tonti within his fortification. But no palisades were there—no smoke ascended from its summit, nor signs of human habitation could be seen. Passing down the rapid current for about two miles, they were surprised to find that the great town of the west had disappeared. The large meadow, only a few months before covered with lodges and swarming with human beings, was now a lonely waste, a representative of death and desolation. On the charred poles which had formed the frame-work of lodges, were many human heads, partly robbed of flesh by birds of prey. Gangs of wolves fled at their approach, and flocks of buzzards raised from their hideous repast, and flew away to distant trees.

Even the burying ground showed marks of the vindictive malice of the conquerors, they having made war on the dead as well as the living. Graves had been opened and bones taken out and piled up in heaps, or broken into fragments and scattered over the prairie. The scaffolds which contained dead bodies, had been torn down and their contents thrown hither and thither on the prairie. Everywhere the blackened ground was strewn with mangled bodies and broken bones of the unfortunate Illinoians. The caches had been broken open, the corn taken out and burned by the victors.

In the midst of these ruins the conquerors had erected an altar to the god of war, and the poles surrounding it were capped with heads of victims whose long hair and ghastly features were sickening to look upon. The stench arising from putrefaction was so offensive, and the scene so horrifying, that La Salle and his party turned away from it, and encamped for the night on the opposite side of the river. During the long winter night the loneliness was increased by the howling of wolves, and buzzards winging their flight back and forth through the dark domain.

On the following morning La Salle returned to the ruined town, and examined the skulls of many of the victims, to see if he could find among them the remains of Tonti and his party, but they all proved to have been the heads of Indians.

On the bank of the river were planted six posts, painted red, and on each of these was a figure of a man drawn in white. La Salle believed these figures represented six white men, prisoners in the hands of Indians, it being the number of Tonti's party.

La Salle and his companions again boarded their canoes and started down the river, hoping to learn something in relation to the fate of their comrades, but nothing was discovered.

As the travelers passed down the river, they saw on the island where the squaws and pappooses had taken refuge, many human figures standing erect, but motionless. With great caution they landed from their canoes to examine these figures, and found them to be partly consumed bodies of squaws, who had been bound to stakes and then burned. Fires had been made at their feet, consuming the flesh off their legs and crisping their bodies, but leaving the remains bound to the stakes, standing erect as though in life; poles were stuck into the marsh and pappooses placed thereon, while others were hanging by the neck from limbs of trees, with the flesh partly eaten off their bodies by birds of prey. Among these remains no warriors were found, as they had fled at the approach of the enemy, leaving the squaws and pappooses to their fate. The sight of these dead bodies was so revolting to look upon, that the French turned away from them, not knowing at what moment they too would fall victims to the savage Iroquois.

A few years after this event, according to tradition, Father Zenobe, with others of his countrymen, visited this island and found here a large piece of ground strewn with human bones.

In the summer of 1829 a black man named Adams, built a cabin opposite the upper end of the island at the mouth of Negro creek. In the following spring Mr. Adams discovered many human bones sticking out of the bank on the island, where the dirt had been washed away by the floods. The same thing was noticed by John Clark, Amos Leonard and other early settlers. It appears the bones were covered up by overflowing of the island, and afterward brought to light by washing away of the bank.

CHAPTER VIII.

FORT ST. LOUIS, ROCK FORT, AND LE ROCHER.

It is believed by the people of the west generally that Fort St. Louis was built on Buffalo Rock,
as relics of an ancient fortification were found
here in the early settlement of the country. But
in comparing the various historical accounts of
this fort, as well as French and Indian traditions,
it will appear quite evident that it stood on Starved
Rock, and here its remains can now be seen. In
an old map, drawn in the days of La Salle, and
preserved with the antiquarian collection at Quebec, Fort St. Louis is located on the south side of
the river, whereas Buffalo Rock is on the north
side. The description of this fort, with its sur-
soundings, as given by the explorers and missionaries, would apply very well to Starved Rock, but
will not answer for Buffalo Rock. Fort St. Louis,
Rock Fort and Le Rocher, so often referred to in
history, are, without doubt, all the same place.

In the summer of 1721, thirty-nine years after

Fort St. Louis was built, Charlevoix, a Jesuit priest, visited the Illinois country, and in his journal gives an account of both of these rocks. On Buffalo Rock he found an Indian village, and in the midst of which was a rude fortification, consisting of low earthworks, with stockades constructed of cottonwood poles, and known as Le Fort des Miames. About one league below Buffalo Rock, on the opposite side of the river, is Le Rocher, rising from the water's edge like a castle wall, to the hight of one hundred and fifty feet, and can be ascended at only one point. On this rock, says Charlevoix, La Salle built a fort, and part of its palisades were still standing. The block-house, store-house and dwellings had been burned by the Indians, and everything about the fort was in ruins, although it had been occupied by his countrymen only three years before.*

*A more romantic place for building a fort could not be found in the western country, and for natural defenses or picturesque appearance, it is without a parallel in history. The many remarkable events connected with this old relic of antiquity, if correctly given, would rival the works of fiction, surpassing even the wild romances of feudal times.

The river at this point assumes a new character—no longer a dull, sluggish stream—but is wide, shallow and rapid, and its broad channel divided by many beautiful islands. Some of these islands are now under cultivation, while others are covered with forest trees, the tall cottonwood and out-spreading elms adding beauty and romance to the surrounding scenery.

Some of these islands in the river, together with the land on which Starved Rock stands, belongs to Col. D. F. Hitt, of Ottawa, who entered it nearly forty years ago.

In the spring of 1680, while La Salle with two
companions were on their way from Fort Creve
Ceour to Canada, they stopped at Starved Rock,
and their account of it is the first given in history.
While they were rowing their canoe up the rapid
stream, they noticed on the right shore a remarkable cliff of rocks, rising from the water's edge
and towering above the forest trees.   Landing
from their canoes they ascended this rock, and
found it to be a natural fortress, where but little
labor would be required to make it impregnable,
so that a few soldiers could hold it against a host
of savages.

When La Salle arrived in Canada he sent word
to Tonti to fortify this rock on the Illinois river
and make it his stronghold, as it was more desirable than Fort Creve Ceour.   Although circumstances prevented Tonti from obeying the orders
of his superior, nevertheless a fort was built here
two years afterwards, and around it clustered the
first colony in the Mississippi valley.

In the fall of 1682 La Salle, with about forty
soldiers under his command, commenced building
a fort on the summit of Starved Rock.   The
place of ascending the rock was improved by
breaking off projecting crags and cutting steps
in the steep pathway.   The stunted cedars which
crowned the summit were cut away to make room

for a fortification, and the margin of the rock for about two-thirds of its circumference was encircled by earthworks. Timbers were cut on the river bottom below, and by hand dragged up the stair-like pathway to build a block-house, a storehouse and dwellings, and protect a large portion of the summit with palisades. A platform was built on the trunks of two leading cedars that stood on the margin of the cliff, and on which a windlass was placed to draw water out of the river for supplying the garrison. All the arms, stores, &c., belonging to the French were carried here and placed within the stockades, and the small cannon, which they had brought in a canoe from Canada, was mounted upon the ramparts.

When the fort was completed the French flag was swung to the breeze, the cannon fired three salutes in honor of Louis XIV, and the soldiers shouted *Vive le roi.*

The fort was named St. Louis or Rock Fort, and in dedicating it Father Zenobe called on the Virgin to bless it, to keep it in the true faith, and protect it from the enemies of the cross.

From the wooden ramparts of St. Louis, which were as high and almost as inaccessible as an eagle's nest, the French could look down on the Indian town below, and also on the great meadow which lay spread out before them like a map.

Two years before, this meadow was a scene of
carnage—a waste of death and desolation, blackened by fire and strewn with the ghastly remains
of the slain in an Iroquois victory—but things
were now changed ; Indians to the number of six
thousand had returned, and the river bank for a
mile in extent was covered with lodges. Indians
from the neighboring villages came here to trade,
bringing with them venison, buffalo meat, furs,
&c., to exchange for goods. At one time there
were encamped around the fort not less than
twenty thousand Indians, who came here to trade
and seek protection from their much dreaded enemies—the Iroquois.

La Salle being now established within his
stockades, turned his attention to trading with the
Indians, supplying them with goods and taking
furs in exchange. Emigrants from Canada came
here and settled near the fort, many of whom
were engaged in trade with the Indians. Some
of these adventurers married squaws, lived in the
village with the Indians and adopted their dress,
habits and customs. The colony was named
Louisiana, in honor of the king of France, and
according to a map drawn at that time it included
within its boundaries all the Mississippi valley.
This vast territory La Salle claimed dominion
over by virtue of his patent, and he commenced

dividing it out to his friends, by giving them
permits to trade with the Indians. He authorized Richard Bosley to establish a trading post at
Cahokia, and Phillip De Beuro one at Green Bay,
but compelling them to pay a royalty to him on
all goods sold and furs bought.

TRADE WITH THE INDIANS.

As soon as a trading post was established at
Fort St. Louis, Indians from different parts of the
country came hither to exchange furs and pelts
for goods, which was done at large profit to the
traders. Tomahawks, knives, &c., made of flint
were superseded by those of steel; blankets, as
wearing apparel, took the place of the heavy buffalo robe, and to the same extent guns superseded
bows and arrows. A blanket worth three dollars
in Quebec, would bring one hundred dollars in
furs, and a tomahawk that cost fifty cents would
sell for twenty dollars among the Indians.

Two years after Fort St. Louis was built, La
Salle, leaving Tonti in command, returned to
Canada, and from thence sailed to France. Being
assisted by the court of France, he on the following year, with three ships loaded with emigrants,
sailed to the Gulf of Mexico for the purpose of
establishing a colony at the mouth of the Missis-

sippi river. This enterprise failed, and La Salle was assassinated by some of his own men while on his way to Illinois*

Although La Salle was dead his colony on the Illinois river continued to flourish, and the fur trade became a source of great wealth. For eighteen years this trade was conducted by Tonti and La Frost, the former living at St. Louis, and the latter in Canada. Furs were sent east in canoes, and in a like manner goods for the Indian trade were brought west. In navigating the lakes a number of canoes were lashed together, and with sails hoisted and oars applied, they would coast along the shore. The connection between the lake and Illinois river was effected by crossing the portage through Mud lake, between Chicago and Des Plains river.†

FLIGHT OF INDIANS AND ATTACK OF FORT.

Two years after building Fort St. Louis, it was attacked by a large body of the Iroquois Indians,

*In the summer of 1686, Tonti, at his own expense, with forty men in canoes, descended the river to the Gulf of Mexico, in search of La Salle, but did not succeed in finding him. Again in 1689 he made a like tour in search of the remnant of the colony, and for the purpose of finding the bones of the great explorer in order to carry them back with him; but this expedition, like the other, proved a failure.

†This passage from the Illinois river to Lake Michigan, was known by the Indians long before the French came to the

who held it in siege six days.   Tonti was in command of the fort, which contained at the time fifty French soldiers, and about one hundred Indian allies, and with this small force put the besiegers to flight.

It was a bright clear day in the latter part of May, and the great meadow was green with grass, intermixed with flowers of various hues; the

country, and it was used by the American pioneers in the early settlement of the west.

In the spring of 1826, John Hamlin, a trader at Peoria, having on hand about one hundred barrels of pork, which he had received from settlers in exchange for goods, conceived a novel idea of shipping it to Fort Dearborn, (now Chicago), where a good price could be obtained. He hired a keel boat which had brought emigrants to Peoria, loaded it with pork, and started it up the river in charge of three boatmen. On the following day Mr. Hamlin, accompanied by Elder Walker and Joseph Smith (Dad Joe) started for Fort Dearborn in a small Mackinaw boat loaded with furs. The wind being from the south, with all the sails hoisted the boat went up the river at the rate of ten miles per hour, and overtook the keel boat near the mouth of Bureau creek.

On reaching the rapids it was found impossible to get the loaded keel boat up the strong current, so it was unloaded and taken up empty, and the pork carried up with many loads of the Mackinaw boat. When above the rapids the pork was again loaded into the keel boat, and she continued on her way toward the lake.

At the mouth of Des Plains river the keel boat was unloaded and sent back to Peoria, while the Mackinaw boat continued on her way to Fort Dearborn. After unloading the furs the Mackinaw boat returned to the mouth of Des Plains, and at different loads carried the pork through to the fort.

The Mackinaw boat, when heavily loaded, drew three feet and a half of water, but the streams being high it passed the portage from Des Plains through Mud lake into Chicago river without getting aground.

trees were in full leaf, and the air was fragrant with blossoms of the wild plum and crab-apple; birds were singing among the branches of trees, and squirrels chirping in the thick river timber, while at a distance was heard the sweet notes of the robin and meadow lark. In the shade of the willows and elms on the river bank lay the doe and her fawn, lulled to slumber by the hum of the wild bee and grasshopper.

All was quiet at Fort St. Louis, and the inmates were delighted with the beauty of the surrounding scenery. To the west, in plain view, lay the great town of La Vantum, with its many hundred lodges built along the bank of the river, and around which were collected thousands of human beings. On the race track, above the town, warriors mounted on ponies were practicing horsemanship, while far in the distance squaws were seen engaged in planting corn or gathering greens for their family meal.

It was Sabbath morning, the fourth after Easter; all the inmates of Fort St. Louis were dressed in their best apparel, and seated under the shade of cedars, awaiting religious services. Father Zenobe, dressed in his long black robe, with a large gold cross hanging from his neck, was about to commence services, when a lone Indian was seen on the bottom prairie going westward, and urging his pony forward at the top of its speed.

Father Zenobe after concluding his sermon, was about to administer the sacrament, when the sentinel at the gate fired his gun to give an alarm. At this signal the meeting broke up, and every one ran to his post, thinking that the fort was about to be attacked. On looking in the direction of the town everything appeared in commotion. Warriors mounted on ponies were riding back and forth at full gallop, squaws and pappooses running hither and thither in wild confusion; drums beating, warriors yelling, while the cries and lamentations of the frightened people could be heard even at the fort. Tonti, with three companions, came down from the fort, boarded a canoe, and with all haste proceeded down the river to ascertain the cause of this excitement, and upon his arrival the mystery was explained.

A scout had arrived with the intelligence that a large body of Iroquois were only ten leagues distant and marching on the town. The tragedy of four years previous was fresh in their minds, and fearing a like result caused them to go wild with terror. The chiefs and warriors collected around Tonti, beseeching him to protect them from the scalping knives and tomahawks of their enemies, in accordance with La Salle's promise.

Tonti in reply said that his force was not sufficient to afford them protection, but advised them to collect their warriors and defend the town. The French, who lived in the town with their wives and a few Indian friends, fled to the fort for security, but the warriors, being seized with a panic and fearing another massacre, in great haste fled, some going down the river in canoes, while others mounted their ponies and galloped westward across the country. Soon after their departure the invaders came, two thousand strong, but they found a barren victory, as not one living soul was left in La Vantum.

When the Iroquois found their intended victims had fled, they attacked the fort and held it in siege six days. For a number of days the Indians continued to fire on the fort from a neighboring cliff, but without producing any effect. The fort not returning the fire, emboldened the assailants, and each day they came closer, and occupied the timber near the base of the rock, with the intention, no doubt, of making an assault. But when they were in close range, the guns were brought to bear on them, and they received the fire of both muskets and cannon. Many were killed, others wounded, while the survivors, being stricken with a panic, fled in great haste, leaving their dead and wounded behind.

No Iroquois Indians were ever seen in that vicinity afterwards, and they never made another raid on the Illinoians.

For many days after the Indians were repulsed, the French remained within their fortifications, and did not venture down from the rock until convinced that the enemy had left the country.

CHAPTER IX.

RETURN OF THE VICTORIOUS ARMY.

In the year 1687, Tonti with fifty French soldiers and two hundred Illinois warriors, went to Canada and joined the army of Governor Denonville, in an expedition against the Indians south of Lake Ontario. Denonville's army was victorious; many towns along the Mohawk river were burned and a large number of scalps taken. After this victory, the army returned to Canada where it was disbanded, when Tonti with his soldiers and Indian allies returned to Illinois. On their return they were accompanied by a number of emigrant families, among whom were many women, wives and daughters of traders and soldiers. For weeks the voyageurs in their canoes coasted along the shore of the lakes, and camping at night on its beach without tents to protect them from the inclement weather. On reaching the mouth of Chicago river they ascended it, crossing the portage into Des Plains, and soon this large fleet of canoes was sailing down the Illinois river.

It was a beautiful clear morning in midsummer; the bright silvery rays of the sun reflected from the rippling waters of the river, as it glided swiftly by. The fresh cooling breeze and the songs of the birds added much to the loveliness of the scene. The occupants of Fort St. Louis, after the morning prayer and exhortation by Father Allonez, were collected along the brink of the rock, watching the finny tribe as they sported over the sand and stones in the clear shallow water. While thus engaged they were startled to hear the sound of a bugle up the river, and on looking in that direction were much surprised to see the broad stream covered with canoes, fast approaching the fort. On came this large fleet, with flags flying, drums beating, and the loud cheering of both French and Indians announcing the return of Tonti's victorious army. As this fleet of canoes passed swiftly down the rapid current, the cannon on the fort boomed forth loud peals of welcome to returning friends.

There was great rejoicing at the fort; wives and daughters of soldiers and traders had come thither to join their friends after years of separation, and their meeting was an affecting one.

On the night following the return of Tonti's

army, a wine supper and ball was given in honor of the occasion, and the great hall of the fort rang with songs, jests, music, and other demonstrations of joy. Ladies from the fashionable society of Montreal gave an air of refinement to the ball, and such a gay party was never before witnessed in the wilds of the west. Much wine was drank, music sounded, and the joyous laugh of the dancers rang forth on the clear night air. Father Allonez having spent twenty years among savages in the west, without mingling in refined society, became so overjoyed by the effects of wine and gay party, that his soul was filled with rapture, and as he passed to and fro among the fair ladies, offered to bestow his blessing upon them.

While the French at the fort were enjoying themselves, the Indians at La Vantum were also having a gay time in honor of returning friends. Many of their favorite dogs were killed, a feast prepared, and they danced around the scalps taken in their late expedition. The sound of their drums and the yells of dancers were heard at the fort, and were responded to by the booming of cannon.

TONTI VISITS THE WINNEBAGO COUNTRY.

For a number of years the Winnebagoes of the north had been trespassing on the Illinoians by hunting on their lands. During the winter, Winnebago hunters would go to Lake Weno to collect furs; sometimes visit the Illinois river and kill large quantities of buffalo, and leave their carcasses as food for wolves or to decay upon the prairie. An ill feeling had existed between these tribes for a long time; a number of hunters from each had been killed, and open hostilities were about to commence. The Illinoians were collecting their warriors from the different villages for the purpose of invading the enemy's country, while the Winnebagoes were making preparations for a raid on the towns along the Illinois river.

Tonti, knowing that a war would ruin the fur trade, and perhaps endanger his own fortified position, resolved on a bold scheme to prevent it. Knowing that the Winnebagoes would collect at their principal town located high up on Rock river, about the middle of September, for the purpose of holding their annual feast, resolved to meet them there with his Illinois allies, and adjust all variances.

Tonti, with twenty French soldiers and twenty Illinois chiefs, among whom was Chassagoac, the principal chief of the tribe, all mounted on ponies, started for the Winnebago country. On arriving at their principal town where the different bands had assembled, they were received as friends and

treated with much respect.   The chiefs and warriors collected around the French, most of whom
had never looked upon the face of a white man
before, and regarded them as superior beings.
The visitors were entertained in the council-
house, and feasted on dog meat, honey, and all
the delicious food which the country afforded.
On the following day after their arrival the chiefs
and principal warriors held a religious dance, and
the strange performance greatly amused the
visitors.

The dancers were naked and their bodies
painted, some with white and others with red or
black clay.   On the head of each was a wreath
of turkey feathers and a pair of deer's horns,
causing them to look more like devils than human beings.   At the sound of drums, flutes and
rattling gourds, the dancing commenced, and continued without cessation until the dancers became
exhausted.   As the loud strains of music animated the dancers, they would leap, hop, and jump
up and down in quick succession, with their
mouths open, tongues banging out, and occasionally yelling at the top of their voice*

Peace was made between the tribes, the wam-

---

*This remarkable dance of the Winnebagoes is a religious
exercise, and only performed at their annual feast. I have
witnessed a similar performance among the howling Dervishes
in Grand Cario, Egypt.

pum belt exchanged, and as a pledge of good faith
the Winnebagoes presented Chassagoac, the head
chief, with two of their most beautiful maidens
for wives. With these two maidens astride of
their ponies, and a great variety of presents, Tonti,
with his French companions and Indian allies,
returned to Fort St. Louis.

THE UNSCRUPULOUS PRIEST.

After the brutal assassination of La Salle in
Texas by some of his own men, his brother,
Father Cavelier, a Jesuit priest, with five companions, started for Fort St. Louis, on the Illinois
river. In an old leaky canoe they ascended the
Mississippi, passing the mouth of the Ohio and
Missouri, and at last reached the placid waters of
the Illinois. After two months of hard labor in
forcing their frail craft up the swift current of the
Father of Waters, annoyed by musquitoes, and
suffering from hunger, they at last reached their
destination, where they received a hearty welcome from their countrymen.

On the 14th day of September, 1688, while
rowing their canoe up the rapid current, they
saw on the right bank a high rocky cliff, towering
above the forest trees, and crowned with palisades.
As they drew near, a troop of Indians, headed by
a white man in French uniform, descended from

the rocky fortress and discharged their guns in honor of their arrival, shouting at the same time, *Vive le roi*. The voyageurs landed from their canoe, ascended the cliff, and were within the stockades of Fort St. Louis. Here were block and stone houses, a magazine, and a small chapel, as well as many Indian lodges, occupied by the allies of the French. Father Cavelier, on viewing the scene around him, was so overjoyed that he fell on his knees, and with uplifted hands returned thanks to the Holy Virgin for her guardian care in protecting him from evil in his long and dangerous journey.

At the time Father Cavelier's party arrived at Fort St. Louis, Tonti was absent on a mission of peace in the Winnebago country, but they were kindly received by his lieutenant, Bellefountain. The clothes of the travelers were torn into fragments while rambling through the cane-brakes and *chaparrel*, at the south, so the kind lieutenant supplied them with new apparel out of the garrison stores A fine satin robe, with a gold cross and other sacred emblems, had been sent from France a short time before by the bishop of Rouen, to be presented to the most devoted Jesuit in North America. The priests of Quebec awarded this gift to Father Chrisp, who had spent a long life among the Indians of Lake

Huron, but of late, chaplain at Fort St. Louis. The cloak and gold emblems were sent west, but before they arrived Father Chrisp had died, consequently, they remained at the fort unclaimed. In the presence of all the soldiers, and a large collection of Indians, Bellefountain presented Father Cavelier with these articles, and in return the holy father raised his hands heavenward, invoking God's blessing on all the occupants of Fort St. Louis.

When Tonti returned to the Fort, he was surprised and much delighted to meet with his countrymen, especially the brother of his esteemed friend, La Salle. On inquiring after the health and prospects of La Salle, the unscrupulous priest replied that he had left him in excellent health and spirits, and his new colony at the mouth of the Mississippi was likely to be a great success. The object of the priest in concealing the death of La Salle, was to use his credit in drawing on Tonti for means to carry him to Canada, and from thence to France. Consequently, in his brother's name, he drew on Tonti for four thousand livres worth of furs, which were placed in two canoes, and the party continued on their way toward Canada. On arriving at Quebec, the party sold their furs and with the proceeds of the sale paid their passage to France.

The fate of La Salle, and the imposition prac-
ticed on Tonti by the hypocritical priest and his
companions, was not known at Fort St. Louis
until the following year.

CHASSAGOAC—HIS DEATH AND BURIAL.

For more than fifty years Chassagoac was head
chief of the Illinois Indians, and by them he was
loved, honored and obeyed. Circumstances caused
this chief to figure extensively in history, and by
the early French explorers he is represented as a
noble specimen of his race.   In a letter of Father
Zenobe's to a friend at Quebec, the chief is described as being very large, with high forehead
and sharp, expressive eyes.   In his nose he wore
a large ring made of buffalo horn, and around his
ankles were wreaths of small bells constructed of
turtle shells, while on his head was a crown of
eagle feathers.

In the gallery of Jesuit collection in the city
of Rouen, can now be seen a life-sized portrait of
Chassagoac, which shows him to have been a fine
specimen of his race, physically as well as men-
tally.   Whether the artist painted this portrait
from life or description is not known, but it is a
good representation of the person described in
history.

Father Hennepin in his journal says, Chassagoac for a time was a true disciple of Christ, but afterwards became a child of perdition, having reference no doubt to his plurality of wives, which practice the priest could not persuade him to give up. On account of his Christian faith, and his fidelity to the French colony, the bishop of Rouen sent him many presents, consisting of gold images, crosses, crucifixes, &c. These presents were kept sacred, and no doubt had much to do in strengthening his faith in religion.

It was a bright day in the latter part of the summer of 1714—all was quite at La Vantum—warriors were fishing along the river bank or engaged in shooting at a mark; squaws attending to their domestic affairs or looking after scores of naked children playing in the dirt. All of a sudden the death-knell was heard, throwing the whole town into confusion, when old and young were seen running hither and thither to learn the cause. The great chief, Chassagoac, in the fullness of his years, had fell dead while standing at the entrance of his lodge. For his death all were in mourning, and the wailing and lamentation of the people were heard at the fort nearly two miles distant. On the following day the French at Fort St. Louis, as well as those belonging to the colony, attended the funeral of the fallen chief and gave him a Christian burial.

His many wives, children and grandchildren together with all the warriors of the town, blacked
their faces, and with loud wailing followed the
remains to the grave. Father Felix pronounced
absolution over the body, sprinkling it with holy
water, according to Jesuit custom, and offered
prayers to the Holy Virgin to admit the spirit to
the paradise above.

A grave having been dug on a gravelly knoll
in the rear of the town, the beloved chief, with
all the presents given him by the priest, consisting of gold and silver crosses, images, crucifixes,
&c., were buried with him. A mound was
raised over the grave, on which Father Felix
erected a large cross bearing a Latin inscription.

On a knoll immediately back of the old town
of Utica, the mound which is supposed to have
been raised over Chassagoac is still to be seen, as
well as the cavity in the earth near by from
which the dirt to erect it was taken.

About sixty years ago, Waba, a Pottowatomie
chief of some note, learning from tradition that
valuable trinkets were buried in this mound,
opened it and robbed it of its treasure.

CHAPTER X.

In the year 1684, La Barre, Governor of Canada, being jealous of La Salle's power and influence, concocted a plan to defeat his enterprise, and thereby appropriate to himself and friends the great wealth to be derived from the fur trade. Under a plea that La Salle had forfeited his charter by granting other parties permits to trade with the Indians, sent an army officer, Captain De Bougis, to Illinois with authority to take command of Fort St. Louis. Tonti being in command of the fort, surrendered it to the usurper, who also took possession of all the goods and furs at the trading post. A few months after Captain De Bougis assumed command, he became convinced that he was holding the fort without authority, consequently, he gave it up to Tonti and returned to Canada.

On the following year after De Bougis had relinquished his command of Fort St. Louis, a tall, spare man, calling himself Captain Richard Pilette, made his appearance at the garrison. This man had been a captain in the army, but for some cause was dismissed from service, and in order to retrieve his fortune came west. Pilette remained at the fort a number of days without letting his business be known, but when the proper time came he drew from his pocket a commission, under the governor's seal, authorizing him to take command. Tonti denied the power of the governor to appoint a commander, as the fort was private property—having been built and maintained by La Salle at his own expense, in accordance with a charter from the King of France. In a pompous manner Pilette proclaimed himself commander of Fort St. Louis by virtue of his commission, and addressing the soldiers in a tone of authority, ordered them to lay hold of Tonti and place him under guard. Without making any reply Tonti, with his iron hand, knocked down the would be commander, and at the same time relieving him of three of his front teeth. Before the usurper could regain his feet, the soldiers carried him outside of the gateway, setting him on the rock, and gave him a start downwards. The rock being covered with sleet, Pilette could not recover his footing or stop his descent, but in that position slid to the bottom, tearing his pantaloons into fragments, and bruising himself on the sharp crags of rocks.

Captain Pilette, bruised and bleeding, his clothing torn almost off him while sliding down the rock, made his way to La Vantum, where he found sympathy among his countrymen and their Indian friends. While here he concocted a plan to gain power of the Indians, and secure their trade, in defiance of La Salle's charter and Fort St. Louis. With eighteen Frenchmen and about fifty warriors he went to Buffalo Rock, and on its summit commenced building a fort. Here they built a block-house, a store-house, and surrounded them with earthworks and palisades. Pilette promised the Indians to supply them with goods, war implements, &c., in exchange for furs, and protect them from the Iroquois. Acting upon this promise, a large number of Indians came here and built lodges within the stockades, as well as around it, and in a short time it became a large town. The place took the name of Le Fort des Miamis, and was occupied by the Indians long after the French left the country. The remains of this fort were plain to be seen in the early settlement of the country, and were mistaken for the relics of Fort St. Louis.

Next year after the fort was built, Captain Pilette collected from the Indians two canoe loads

of pelts and furs, which he contemplated shipping
to Canada, and paying for them in goods on his
return.   The captain, with three companions, was
about to start on this journey, when both French
and Indians were collected on the river bank
to bid them adieu. But as their canoes were
about to leave the shore, Tonti, with a file of
armed soldiers, made his appearance and forbid
them going until the duty authorized by La
Salle's charter was paid.   Pilette protested
against being robbed in this way, as he termed it,
but knowing that Tonti with his armed soldiers
would enforce his demand, consented to pay the
tribute.   Accordingly the required number of
buffalo, beaver and otter skins was counted out,
after which the canoes departed on their way

Pilette married a squaw, raised a large family
of half-breed children, to whom he left a large
fortune, which he had made in the fur trade.
When he died they buried him on Buffalo Rock,
and raised a mound over his remains.   A short
distance from the site of the old fort and town,
are a number of small artificial mounds, raised
over the remains of distiguished persons.   For
years these mounds have been plowed over by
A. Betger, the owner of the land, but still their
outlines are plain to be seen.   The largest one of
the group, and standing some distance from the

others, is, in all probability, the one raised over the tomb of Captain Pilette.

After Pilette's death, his family removed to Peoria Lake, and one of his grandsons, Louis Pilette was a claimant for the land on which Peoria is built. Many of the descendants of this old fur trader are now living on the American Bottom, all of whom show strong marks of Indian origin. One of these descendants, Hypolite Pilette, a great grandson of the Captain, has in his possession a number of articles which once belonged to his distinguished grandsire. From this man I obtained most of the traditionary account of Le Fort des Miamis, as well as many other facts relating to the French and Indians of that day.

STRANGE INDIAN CUSTOMS.

The Illinois Indians like many of the western tribes, were divided into clans, which were designated by names of animals, such as wolf, bear, buffalo, deer, &c. In the marriage relation these clans were observed and their conditions strictly complied with. A warrior was not allowed to take a wife of his own clan, but could make his selection from a different one. Thus wolf could not marry wolf, but could marry bear, buffalo or deer.

The chieftainship was hereditary, but not always in a direct line. Thus, a son of a chief may not inherit his title and authority; although a reputed heir he may not be a natural one, but the son of the chief's daughter is always preferred, as most likely to be of royal blood.

The Indians believed that sickness was caused by a demon or evil spirit taking possession of the patient, and the physician, who being a sorcerer, would expel it by charms or incantations. This he would do by songs, beating his drum, yelling at the top of his voice, and sometimes hissing like a serpent. If the case was a bad one, and the demon could not be expelled by mild means, more powerful ones were resorted to. In stubborn cases the physician would beat, choke and pinch his patients, sometimes biting them until the blood would flow; whoop and yell over him, and rattle tortoise shells in his ears. But if all this failed to drive out the evil spirit, a council of the patient's friends is called, a fire built, and the sick person burned upon it, so the demon might not escape and get into some one else.

Some of the dead were buried in the ground, while others were wrapped in buffalo robes and placed on scaffolds, out of the reach of wolves. Here the body remained until the flesh decayed, then the bones were taken down and laid away in a grave. Sometimes the remains of persons killed in a battle or by accident, were boiled, the flesh taken off and the bones laid away in one corner of the lodge until the time came for a public burial. It was the custom to bury the chiefs in some favorite spot, and raise a mound over them to perpetuate their memory, and on the fifth day of the tenth moon of each year, the warriors with their faces blacked, would meet at the grave and moan over the departed.

On the prairie near the old town of Utica, some of these mounds are still to be seen, and they have been noticed near the site of other Indian villages of the west.

Infants after death were wrapped in a deer skin, placed in a trough covered with bark and hung to the limb of a tree, where they were left to be swung back and forth by the wind. For many days after the death of an infant, the bereaved mother would go at sunset and seat herself at the root of the tree, and for hours at a time, sing to the sleeping babe, sweet lullaby.

MANITOS AND BARSES.

The Illinois Indians believed in a great spirit called Manito, that lived in the skies and governed heaven and earth. Besides this great spirit, there were many smaller ones, that resided in rocks or

caves of the earth, and would appear in the form
of a fairy or a big white bird; sometimes as a
rabbit or fawn. Great efforts were made by both
old and young to keep on good terms with these
good spirits, as they protected them from the
evil ones.

Young warriors at the age of fifteen would
paint their faces, cover their heads with an elk or
coon skin, and retire to a lonely place where they
would remain two days and nights, fasting and
praying for the manifestations of their Manito,
which was sure to appear to them in a dream.
Sometimes this spirit would appear to them in
the form of a bird, a rabbit, antelope, or buffalo,
and follow them through life, acting as a guardian
angel, protecting them from the powers of the
evil one. In whatever form the good spirit man-
ifested itself, must be represented by a corres-
ponding idol, which is carried with them at all
times. When starting on the war-path, each
warrior puts his protector, called *Totem*, which is
generally a skin of a snake, a tail of a buffalo, a
horn of a deer, claw of a coon, or the head of an
eagle, into a medicine bag. This medicine bag is
carried by a priest or medicine man, who leads
the way, and the warriors follow after him in
single file.

The Indians believed in many evil spirits, some

of large and others of small magnitude. These
spirits or demons, called *barses*, were all the while
roaming through the earth in search of prey, attacking and destroying all persons unprotected
by a good spirit. The smaller ones would frequently appear in the form of a serpent, a turtle,
or a wolf, but the larger ones, whose size exceeds
that of a horse or buffalo, with a long tail and
cloven feet, and whose roar during a thunder
storm could be heard miles away, and would attack and destroy all persons unprotected.

About two miles south of La Vantum, in the
thick timber of the Big Vermillion, is a singular
rocky chasm or canon, extending from the creek
about eighty rods back into the bluff, and now
known as Deer Park. At the upper end of this
canon is a waterfall, caused by a small stream
falling from the projecting rock. Under this
waterfall was once a large cavern, but long since
closed up by the settling of the rock, and at present scarcely perceptible. According to Indian
tradition, in this rocky cavern once lived a great
demon in the form of a buffalo, with immense
horns that folded up on his back, and a tail of
great length which he would swing to and fro
over his body. This great demon or barse was
frequently seen by the Indians during the night,
while passing to and from his den, and for many

years no one would go into Vermillion timber to hunt for fear of being devoured by him.

During the dead hours of the night, while the wind blew and thunder roared, this demon could be heard howling round the town. At one time he produced frost in midsummer, which destroyed all the corn, and at other times knocked it all down with the force of his breath.

During the dead hours of night, this evil spirit would assume the form of a man, enter lodges while all were alseep, and breathe poison into the nostrils of the sleepers, causing many to sicken and die. Sometimes he would steal unborn infants from their mother's womb, and by him young maidens were robbed of their virtue.

CHRISTIANIZING THE INDIANS.

The Jesuits of North America, whose headquarters was in Quebec, made great efforts to Christianize the Illinois Indians, and for that purpose many missionaries were sent west, who carried with them gold and silver emblems of their religion. These missionaries abandoned all the comforts of civilization, and spent their days in wigwams with the wild sons of the forest, all for the glory and honor of the Redeemer. But all their labors availed nothing, as the Indians conformed to the modes of Christian worship only

for the gifts they expected to receive. Many
made an open profession of Christianity, observed
its form, but in fact still retained their own prin-
ciples of religion. The Jesuits were zealous in
their work of proselyting, impressing on the
minds of the Indians, that without Christian baptism they would be cast into a lake which burneth
with fire and brimstone. But the Indians had
been taught from their infancy, that when overtaken by death they would be conducted by a
good spirit to the happy hunting grounds, to join
their friends who had gone before them, and their
early convictions the priest could not remove.

All those who were baptized the priest pronounced saved from perdition, and their names
were enrolled in the great book of the church.
They counted the conversions by the number of
baptisms, when in fact it had but little to do with
it, as many were willing to be baptized every day
in the week for a pint of whisky or a pound of
tobacco.

The medals, crosses and crucifixes which the
Jesuits gave the warriors, pleased their fancy, as
they were fond of adorning their person with
glittering trinkets. And with these representa-
tions of man's salvation suspended from their
necks, they would remain heathens still. In ad-
dition to decorating their persons with tokens of

Christianity, many of the warriors wore necklaces made of dried fingers taken from an enemy, whom they had slain in battle. The former represented their religion, and the latter their patriotism.

Marquette appears to have been an exception to all other Jesuits who labored for the conversion of the Indians. While others failed, his efforts were crowned with success, and he made many converts wherever he went. Long after his death his memory was held sacred, and the places which he visited hallowed by posterity.

CHAPTER XI.

For a period of fifteen years after the death of
La Salle, the trade with the Illinois Indians was
carried on by Tonti and La Frost, under special
charter from the king of France. La Frost spent
most of his time in Canada, while Tonti remained
at Fort St. Louis, shipping each year a large
quantity of furs, and receiving goods in exchange.
In the year 1702, the Governor of Canada, claim-
ing that these traders had forfeited their charter
by collecting furs at various points on Lake Michigan, and by military force he took possession of
Fort St. Louis, confiscating to the government all
their stock in trade. By this act of injustice
Tonti was not only disgraced by the arbitrary
power of the governor, but was ruined in fortune.
Calling his friends together, he took leave of them,
saying that he was about to depart from the
country never to return. Both French and Indians collected around Tonti, beseeching him to

remain with them, but he had resolved to do otherwise, and with tears in their eyes he bade them adieu. Accompanied by two companions, he boarded a canoe and started down the river in search of new adventures.

On reaching the lower Mississippi, Tonti joined D'Iberville, and assisted him in establishing a colony in that country. For sixteen years he remained south, part of the time entrusted with important missions, but when the colony was broken up by sickness and Spanish invasion, he became an outcast and a wanderer. Broken down in health, and feeling that his end was nigh, he employed two Indians to take him to Fort St. Louis, so he could once more look upon the scene of his vigor and manhood, and leave his bones among the people by whom he had long been honored and obeyed.

It was a warm afternoon in the early part of August, 1718, when the occupants of Fort St. Louis were lounging around the palisades, under the shade of evergreens, some sleeping and others engaged in games of dice and checkers, when they discovered a canoe coming up the river rowed by two Indians. In the bottom of the canoe lay a man on a buffalo robe, but as they came nigh the fort he raised himself into a sitting position, and gazed wildly around him. The

canoe landed at the base of the rock, and the
Indians dragged it on shore to prevent its being
carried away by the current.   After securing their
canoe they commenced ascending Starved Rock,
when their strange appearance caused many con-
jectures among the inmates of the fort.   Between
the two Indians was a feeble old man, whom the
conductors held by each arm, and were slowly
assisting him up the rocky pathway.   On reaching the fort at the summit of the rock, the old
man was placed on a bunk, where he lay for some
time unable to speak, being exhausted by the
fatigue of the journey.   After taking some stim-
ulants his energies revived, and he inquired of
those around him who commanded the fort.   On
being told it was Captain La Mott, he gave a
heavy sigh, saying that La Mott was a usurper,
and he the rightful commander.   The people
thought him crazy or his mind wandering, and
they bathed his head with cold water.   When
sufficiently recovered from exhaustion, he told
them that he was Tonti, and come here to die.
The old man's statements, although at first dis-
credited by most of those present, created much
excitement among the soldiers, but when convinced of its truthfulness, one after another came
forward and embraced him.

Sixteen years had made a great change in the

appearance of Tonti, and he was scarcely recognized by his most intimate friends. His tall manly form was bent by disease, his piercing black eyes were dimmed with age, and his raven black hair was now white as snow.

News of Tonti's arrival at Fort St. Louis spread throughout the country, and the French, half-breeds and Indians at the different villages came to see him. But, alas, those who had known him while in the vigor of manhood, could scarcely be convinced that the feeble old man that they now beheld was once the proud, brave and fearless Tonti of former years.

A few days after Tonti arrived at the fort he took the sacrament at the hands of a priest, and while looking upon a gold crucifix which was held before his face, he breathed his last. A grave was dug on the river bank, close to the west end of Starved Rock, in which his remains found a long resting place.

For many years after Tonti's death, both French and Indians while passing up and down the river would stop to visit his grave, and sometimes place upon it flowers or mementoes in memory of him who sleeps beneath.

FORT ST. LOUIS BURNED AND COLONY BROKEN UP.

So long as the fur trade was conducted by Tonti

and La Frost, the Indians were well pleased with their manner of doing business, but when it came under the supervision of the Governor of Canada, a new order of things was introduced, which caused much dissatisfaction. The governor appointed unscrupulous agents to conduct the trade, who swindled the Indians by selling them worthless articles, such as counterfeit jewelry, knives, tomahawks, &c., made of pot-metal. These traders paid the government a certain duty on all pelts shipped to Canada, and no one was allowed to trade with the Indians unless authorized to do so by the governor. The duty consisted of a certain number of skins out of each cargo, which the traders compelled the Indians to furnish, otherwise their value was deducted on making payment. The Indians being imposed upon by these swindlers, an unfriendly feeling sprung up up between them.

There were other causes of ill feeling between the French and Indians, among which was the marriage relation. A Frenchman having married a young squaw would put her away as soon as he found another one more attractive, thus changing his wife at will according to his fancy. Although the priests would not tolerate bigamy among their countrymen, yet they were willing to accept a marriage fee once a month, twice a week, or as often as the applicant desired a new wife. The young squaws were fond of beads, rings and other trinkets, with which they would adorn their persons, and the one giving them the most presents they were willing to marry. It was the hight of their ambition to marry a white man, notwithstanding they were liable to be put away at any time, if their lord found one more attractive than themselves.

Under the Indian code of morals, a squaw, if found unchaste, was punished by cutting off one ear or branded on the forehead, but there was no law to prevent them marrying every day in the week, or as often as an opportunity occurred.

Captain La Mott was now in command of the fort, and being a man fond of pleasure, and devoid of conscientious scruples, converted it into a regular harem, in open violation of both the French and Indian code of morals. Young Indian maidens were in the habit of spending their nights at the fort, under the pretext of being married to soldiers, returning home in the morning with their heads adorned with worthless trinkets, and their minds poisoned by vile associations. The squaws became so facinated with the French that many refused to marry among their own people, and had come to the conclusion that their children were not worth raising, unless they had

French blood in their veins. Things had come to such a state in their social relations, that the head chief, Jero, called a council of chiefs and warriors, and at which it was agreed to expel the French from among them.

On a warm morning in the latter part of the summer of 1718, while most of the occupants of Fort St. Louis, after a night of revelry and debauchery, were still asleep in their bunks, when suddenly aroused by the presence of the avengers. Captain La Mott, awakening from his morning nap, was astonished on being confronted by about three hundred warriors, armed and painted as for war. The Captain inquired the object of their visit, when Jero, the head chief, informed him that they were here to destroy the fort. The chief ordered the warriors to fire the buildings, and in a few moments the block-house, store-house and dwellings were in flames, all of which were burned to the ground. Thus Fort St. Louis was destroyed, after standing thirty-six years, and being the head-center of the French settlement in Illinois.

On the destruction of the fort the colony was broken up; some of the traders returned to Canada, others to the French settlement at Cahokia, but the greater portion to Peoria Lake, where a colony had been established seven years before.

Three years after the burning of Fort St. Louis, Charlevoix visited Illinois, and found the palisades still standing. No Frenchmen lived here at that time, but in the great town near by were seen scores of half-breed children.

Some years ago Gen. Cass brought from France a manuscript, dated 1726, and relates to western Indians. It speaks of a war existing between the Illinoians and Sacs, and Foxes, of Green Bay. It also refers to M. De Siette, commander in Illinois, and of the propriety of calling a council at Chicago, or at the Rock, undoubtedly meaning Starved Rock.

RELICS OF FORT ST. LOUIS.

In the summer of 1805, a party at Kaskaskia, learning from tradition that a large amount of gold had been buried within the stockades of Fort St. Louis, went in search of it. At that time the location of Fort St. Louis was unknown. History and tradition alike failed to point it out; but they knew it was on a rock washed by the rapid current of the Illinois, and a short distance above the great bend in the river. On Buffalo Rock they found as they supposed relics of the fort, and here they spent a number of days in searching for the hidden treasure. But finding nothing, they returned home and published an account of their expedition in the newspapers of that day. In this account they describe the remains of the fort on a large rock, located on the north side of the river, and from that time forward it was conceded that Fort St. Louis was built on Buffalo Rock.

It has already been shown that Buffalo Rock did not answer the description of the place spoken of in history, but the natural advantages between these two rocks for a fortification, could not escape the observation of a man with La Salle's shrewdness. Buffalo Rock contains on its summit several hundred acres of land, is only about sixty feet high, and accessible at various points, consequently it would require a large force to hold a fort thus located. Whereas, Starved Rock is one hundred and thirty-six feet high, contains on its summit less than one acre, can only be reached at one point, which makes it a natural fortress, where but little labor would be required to make it impregnable, so that a few soldiers could hold it against all the savages of the west.

Immediately south of Starved Rock, and about one hundred and fifty yards distant, is a high cliff of rocks, isolated from the neighboring cliffs, and known as Devil's Nose. Eastward, across a chasm two hundred and fifty yards in width, and covered

with a thick growth of timber, is another rocky
cliff of equal hight. This cliff rises almost per-
pendicularly from the water's edge, connecting
with the main bluff, and from an old Indian
legend is called Maiden's Leap. These two cliffs
are almost as high as Starved Rock, and if occupied by the assailants would be within gunshot
of the fort. Therefore, it became necessary to
protect the sides next to them with earthworks
and palisades. The earthworks on the sides next
to these cliffs, enclosing almost two-thirds of the
circumference of the rock, are still to be seen,
leaving that next to the river without any protection whatever, as none were here needed. These
works commence at the western angle, following
the margin of the rock (which is of a circular
form) to the extreme east, leaving an open gateway on the south, where the path ascends the
rock, and is one hundred and twenty-two yards
in length. On the south side of the rock and all
along the earthworks, which are now covered
with small trees and stunted evergreens, are many
pit-holes, two of which are very large. It is
quite probable that one of these was the magazine of the garrison, and the other a cellar of
the store-house. The smaller pit-holes, which
are seen here and there among the bushes,
according to tradition, were dug forty-seven years

after Fort St. Louis was destroyed, and under the
following circumstances:

When the Governor of Canada took possession
of Fort St. Louis, all the goods and furs belonging
to the traders were confiscated to the government
and report says divided between the governor and
his friends.   Tonti, having at the time, in his
possession a large amount of gold, dug a hole
within the stockades and buried it to prevent its
falling into the hands of the governor.   Sixteen
years afterwards, as Tonti was about breathing
his last, he told a priest who was holding a gold
crucifix before his face, about the gold being
buried within the fort.   The priest kept the matter
a secret, waiting for an opportunity to resurrect
the gold, but soon after he was drowned in the
river by the upsetting of a canoe.   The fort was
also burned and the French driven away, as previously stated.

In the summer of 1765, forty-seven years after
Fort St. Louis was abandoned, a party of French
at Peoria, among whom were Captain De Fond
and Father Buche, believing the story about gold
being buried in the fort, came up the river in
search of it.   They encamped at the base of
Starved Rock, and spent many days in digging
on its summit.   No gold was found, but in a vault
near where the store-house had stood, they found

a large number of articles designed for the Indian trade, consisting of tomahawks, knives, beads, guns and other articles. The digging for gold on Starved Rock accounts for the many pit-holes now to be seen.

This account of searching for gold is given in Father Buche's manuscript, now in possession of Hypolite Pilette, and from which many extracts are taken. Said he, "We had spent five days in digging pit-holes on the summit of Le Rocher, and found a large quantity of articles which were intended for the Indian trade, but the precious metal—the object of our search—we found none. On the last day of our stay we dug a hole close to the old earthwork, and continued working until it was quite dark, when the devil appeared to us in the form of a huge bear. On seeing this monster we dropped our tools and hurried down from the rock, put our camp kit in the canoe and started down the river."

This story of gold being buried within the stockades of Fort St. Louis, is also among the Indian traditions, and some years ago a party of Pottawatomies from Western Kansas came here to search for it. People told them that Fort St. Louis was built on Buffalo Rock, and on it they dug a number of pit-holes, but finding nothing they returned to their homes.

CHAPTER XII.

FRENCH SETTLEMENT AT PEORIA.

At what time the French commenced a settlement at Peoria, has long been a controverted point on which history and tradition are alike defective. Some believe it commenced when La Salle built Fort Creve Ceour, in the year 1680, and from that time people continued to reside here. Others fix the permanent settlement of the place about the year 1760; but from an old letter in the possession of a descendant of an early pioneer, as well as traditionary accounts, it is quite evident that it commenced at an early period. I have given this subject much attention by gathering up scraps of history relating to it, and by conversing with many of the descendants of the Peoria French, some of whom trace their genealogy back to the days of La Salle. By comparing these different accounts it is shown conclusively that the settlement at Peoria commenced in the year 1711, and under the following circumstances:

In the summer of 1711, Father Marest, a Jesuit priest from Canada, preached to the Indians at Cahokia, and by the force of his eloquence a large number of them were converted to Christianity. Among these converts was a chief named Kolet, from Peoria, who at the time was at Cahokia, visiting friends. The chief prevailed on Father Marest to accompany him home to his village at Peoria Lake, and proclaim salvation to his people. Late in November the priest and chief, accompanied by two warriors, started in a bark canoe for Peoria, but after going ten leagues the river froze up, so that further progress by water was out of the question; therefore the travelers hid their canoe, with most of their baggage, in the thick river timber, and continued their journey on foot.

For twelve days they waded through snow and water, crossing big prairies and through thick timber, full of briars and thorns. Sometimes crossing marshes and streams where the ice would give way, letting them into water up to their necks. At night they slept on dry grass or leaves, gathered from under the snow, without shelter or anything but their blankets to protect them from the cold winter blast. The provisions for their journey, as well as their bedding, was left with their canoe, consequently they were obliged to subsist on wild grapes and game killed by the way. After many days of fatigue and exposure, their limbs frost bitten, and their bodies reduced in flesh from starvation, they at last reached the village, and from the natives received a hearty welcome.

This Indian village (afterwards called Opa by the French) was situated on the west bank of Peoria Lake, one mile and a half above its outlet. On La Salle's first visit to this place, thirty-one years before, he found here a large town, and was cordially received by the head chief, Niconope. This chief had long since been gathered to his fathers, and his place was occupied by Kolet, above referred to.

Father Marest found quarters in an Indian lodge, and remained in the village until spring without meeting with one of his countrymen. He preached to the Indians almost daily, many of whom embraced Christianity, and their names were afterwards enrolled in the church book.

On the following spring the French at Fort St. Louis established a trading post at Peoria Lake, and a number of families came thither from Canada and built cabins in the Indian village. For fifty years the French and half-breeds continued to live in the town with the Indians, and during that period peace and harmony prevailed among them. But in course of time this town was abandoned for one that figured extensively in its day, and known in history as

LA VILLE DE MAILLET.

In the summer of 1761, Robert Maillet, a trader of Peoria, built a dwelling one mile and a half below the town, near the outlet of the lake, and moved his family thither. Here the land rises gradually from the water's edge until it reaches the high prairie in the rear, forming a beautiful sloping plateau, unequalled by any spot on the Illinois river. This locality for a town was considered preferable to the old one, the ground being dryer, the water better, and it was considered more healthy, consequently, others came and built houses by the side of Maillet's. The inhabitants gradually deserted the old town for the new one, and within a few years the latter became a place of great importance. No French lived in the old town after the year 1764, but for many years it remained an Indian village, and the houses vacated by the French, were occupied by the natives until they rotted down.

The new town took the name of La Ville de Maillet (that is Maillet's village), after its proprietor, and was in existence fifty-one years. A fort was built on high ground, overlooking the lake on one side, and the sloping prairie on the other. This fort consisted of two large block-houses, surrounded by earthworks and palisades, with an open gateway to the south next to the town, and was only intended as a place of retreat in case of trouble with the Indians. The fort was never occupied except a short time by Robert Maillet, who used one of the block-houses for a dwelling, and the other for the sale of goods. Some years afterwards, Maillet left the fort for a more desirable place of residence and trade, and it remained vacant for many years, the enclosure within the stockades being used by the citizens in common for a cow-yard.

In 1820 Hypolite Maillet, in testifying in the United States Court, in a suit brought on French claims, said that he was forty-five years old, and was born in a stockade fort which stood near the southern extremity of Peoria Lake.

In the winter of 1788, a large party of Indians came to Peoria for the purpose of trade, and in accordance with their former practice, took quarters in the old fort. They purchased a cask of brandy for the purpose of having a spree. All got drunk, had a war dance, and during their revelry set the block-houses on fire and burned them down.

When the Americans commenced a settlement at Peoria, in the spring of 1819, the outlines of the old French fort were plain to be seen on the high ground, near the lake, and a short distance above the present site of the Chicago and Rock Island depot. The line of earthworks could be traced out by the small embankments, and in some places pieces of pickets were found above ground. Back of the fort was the remains of a blacksmith shop, and near by grew a wild plum tree. This plum tree was dug up by John Brisket, the owner of the land, and under it was fouud a vault containing a quanty of old metal, among which were a number of gun-barrels, knives, tomahawks, copper and brass trinkets, &c. Among other things found in this vault, were pieces of silver and brass plate for inlaying gun-stocks, ornamenting knife-handles, &c. These things appeared to be the stock in trade of a gunsmith, and for some cause unknown were buried here.*

According to the statements of Antoine Des Champs, Thomas Forsyth and others, who had long been residents of Peoria previous to its destruction in 1812, we infer that the town contained a large population. It formed a link between the settlements of Kaskaskia, Cahokia and Canada, and being situated in the midst of

* "Ballance's History of Peoria."

an Indian country, caused it to be a great place of fur trade. At one time it contained about sixty houses, besides many lodges occupied by Indians part of the year. The town was built along the beach of the lake, and to each house was attached an out-lot for a garden, which extended back some distance on the prairie. The houses were all constructed of wood, some with frame work and sided up with split timber, while others were built with hewed logs, notched together after the style of a pioneer's cabin. The floors were laid with puncheons, and the chimney built with mud and sticks.

General Clark conquered Illinois and took possession of the settlements at Kaskaskia and Cahokia in 1778, after which he sent three soldiers with two French Creoles, in a canoe to Peoria to notify the people that they were no longer under British rule, but citizens of the United States. Among these soldiers was a man named Nicholas Smith, afterwards a resident of Bourbon county, Kentucky, and whose son, Joseph Smith, (Dad Joe) was the among the first American settlers at Peoria. Through this channel we have an account of Peoria as it appeared almost a century ago, and which agrees well with other traditionary accounts.

Mr. Smith said Peoria, at the time of his visit

was a large town, built along the beach of the lake, with narrow, unpaved streets, and houses constructed of wood. Back of the town were gardens, stock-yards, barns, &c., and among these was a wine press with a large cellar or underground vault for storing wine. There was a church with a large wooden cross rising above the roof, and gilt lettering over the door. There was an unoccupied fort on the bank of the lake, and close by it was a wind-mill for grinding grain. The town contained six stores or places of trade, all of which were well filled with goods for the Indian market. The inhabitants consisted of French half-breeds and Indians, not one of whom could speak or understand English.

FRENCH INHABITANTS OF PEORIA.

The inhabitants of Peoria consisted of French Creoles, emigrants from Canada, and half-breeds. Many of them intermarried with the natives, so that their posterity at the present time show strong marks of Indian origin. They were a peaceable, quiet people, ignorant and superstitious, and influenced very much by the priests. They had no public schools, and but few of them except priests and traders, could read or write. Out of eighteen claimants for the land where Peoria stands, all

but three signed their names with a mark.
Among the inhabitants were merchants or traders
who made annual trips to Canada in canoes, carrying thither pelts and furs, and loading back
with goods for the Indian market. There were
mechanics among them, such as blacksmiths,
wagon-makers, carpenters, &c.; and most of the
implements used in farming and building were of
home manufacture. Although isolated from the
civilized world, and surrounded by savages, their
standard of morality was high ; theft, murder and
robbery was seldom heard of. They were a gay,
joyous people, having many social parties, wine
suppers and balls ; living in harmony with the
Indians, who were their neighbors and friends,
and in trading with them they accumulated most
of their wealth.

The French settled at Peoria without a grant
or permission from any government, and the title
to their lands was derived from possession only.
But these titles were valid according to usages, as
well as a village ordinance, and lands were bought
and sold the same as if patented by government.
Each person had a right to claim any portion of
the unoccupied land, and when in possession his
title was regarded sacred. Every settler had a
village lot for a garden attached to his residence,
and if a farmer, a portion in the common field.

On the prairie west of the town were extensive farms, all enclosed in one field, each person contributing his share of fencing, and the time of securing the crops and pasturing the stock, was regulated by a town ordinance. The boundaries of these farms could be traced out in the early settlement of Peoria, as the lands showed marks of having been cultivated. When a young man married, a village lot, and a tract of land in the common field (if a farmer) was assigned to him, and it was customary for the citizens to turn out and build him a house.

The inhabitants of Peoria had extensive vineyards, and each year made a large quantity of wine, much of which they traded to the Indians in exchange for furs. They domesticated the buffalo and crossed them with native cattle, which was found to improve the stock. These cattle could live during the winter without the expense of feeding, but while buffalo remained in the country they lost many by straying off with the herd. On the following summer, after the French were driven away from Peoria, a party of adventurers from St. Clair county came here and drove a large number of these cattle home with them. These cattle were highly prized by the inhabitants, as they would winter on the American Bottoms without having to feed them. This stock of cattle was known here for many years, and at the present time some of their off-spring show marks of buffalo origin, and their hides are frequently tanned for robes.*

When a settlement was commenced at Peoria, the country belonged to France, afterwards to Great Britain, and lastly to the United Ststes. When Illinois came under British rule in 1756, Captain Stirling, commanding at Kaskaskia, sent a messenger to Peoria to notify them that they were British subjects. Afterwards, when Illinois by conquest came under United States authority, they were again notified of a change in government, but they still remained French in feeling and sympathy. They claimed no allegiance to any government, paid no taxes, and acknowledged no law except their own village ordinance. While these people were living in peace and harmony,

---

*For one hundred years after the French made a settlement in the west, no horses except Indian ponies were used by them, and for the first thirty years cattle and hogs were unknown. Tradition says two young pigs were brought in a canoe from Canada to Fort St. Louis, and from these hogs were raised to supply the setttlements on the Mississippi. At Cahokia the settlers caught a number of buffalo calves, and raised them with the expectation of domesticating them, but it proved a failure, for they went off with a herd of wild ones.

It is said when Crozat obtained a patent for the Illinois country, in 1771, then called Louisiana, his agent, Colonel De Mott, employed two half-breeds to drive a herd of cattle through the wilderness from Cana to Kaskaskia, and from these originated the stock in the Mississippi valley.

being two hundred miles from the nearest point of civilization, they were attacked by an armed force, their town burned and the heads of families carried off prisoners of war, as will be narrated in a subsequent chapter. There are many incidents related, showing that trouble existed at different times between the French and their red neighbors, among which are the following:

In the year 1781, a Frenchman killed an Indian with whom he had trouble, and for a time all the white population were threatened with destruction. A large party of warriors came to Peoria and demanded the murderer, but he could not be found, having fled down the river, as was afterwards shown. But the Indians believed that the murderer was secreted by his friends, so they gave the French three days to deliver him up, and if not forthcoming at the specified time they would burn the town. This caused a great panic; some fled for Cahokia, others took quarters in the fort, but before the time had expired, the Indians were convinced that the murderer had fled, consequently pledges of friendship were renewed.

Again, in 1790, about five hundred warriors came to Peoria and demanded the surrender of a certain trader, whom they accused of causing the murder of Pierre de Beuro, but finally left without him.

CHAPTER XIII.

PONTIAC.

Probably no North American Indian has acquired so much fame and notoriety, and whose power was so much felt in the early settlement of the country, as Pontiac. This Indian, to whom historians so often refer, was born and raised near Detroit, and for many years was head chief of the Ottawas. Like Phillip, of Mount Hope, his power and influence extended over neighboring tribes, and he was more like a king than a chief. So long as the French held dominion over the west, and conducted the trade of the lake country, Pontiac lived on friendly terms with them, but when it came in posession of the British, he denounced the latter as enemies to his people, and made an effort to drive them from the country. While Major Rogers, of the British army, was marching westward with a regiment of soldiers, for the purpose of taking possession of Detroit, he was met by Pontiac, who inquired by what authority he was passing through his country. With his tall figure raised to its full hight, and while holding his right hand before the face of the British commander, he said to him, "I stand in your path, and you can go no further without my permission."

However, Pontiac allowed the British to take possession of the French trading posts along the lakes, and for a time professed to be friendly toward them. But a few years afterwards he made war against the red coats and tried to drive them from the country. He united with him all the neighboring tribes, forming what is known in history as Pontiac's Conspiracy, and a long and bloody war resulted.

In order to carry on the war, this great chief issued checks cut out of birch bark, calling for various amounts, payable in furs. These checks were taken by different tribes in payment for munitions of war, and all of which were redeemed according to agreement.

Pontiac was an Indian of gigantic statue; a towering intellect, and exercised almost unlimited power over his followers. He pretended to commune with the Great Spirit, who on one occasion said to him: "Why do you let these dogs in red clothing take possesion of your country; rise in your might and drive them from the land."

Pontiac, in an address to his warriors, said: "Although the red coats have conquered the French, they have not conquered us. We are not slaves nor squaws, and as long as the Great Spirit is our ruler, we will maintain our rights. These lakes, and these woods were given us by our fathers, and we will part with them only with our lives."

For a long time Pontiac was victorious, but at last the fortune of war turned against him; then his allies forsook his cause and made peace with the British. On being betrayed by his allies, he fled from the country and found refuge on the Kankakee river, a short distance above its junction with the Illinois. In his fight from Michigan he was accompanied by about two hundred warriors, with their squaws and pappooses. With this remnant of his band he formed an alliance with the Pottawatomies, who, at that time, occupied the lake and Wabash counties, and from thenceforth they became one tribe.

Pontiac, by locating his band on Kankakee river, gave offense to the Illinois Indians, who were the owners of the land; consequently, Kineboo, the head chief, accompanied by a retinue of warriors, mounted on ponies, went to the Ottawa camp, where they found the new comers engaged in building lodges and making prepara-

tions to plant corn.   Kineboo notified them that
they were trespassers, and gave them two moons
to leave the country, but if found there at the
expiration of that time, he would remove them
by force.   But when the Illinoians found that the
Ottawas were backed by the powerful tribe of
Pottawatomies, they did not molest them.

MASSACRE OF A HUNTING PARTY.

During the summer season the buffalo, on account of the green-headed flies, would leave the
Wabash country and the prairies on the east part
of the State, and range west and north of the
Illinois river.   Consequently, buffalo were seldom seen south and east, while the prairies to the
westward, for miles in extent, were frequently
blackened with large herds of them.   On this
account the Pottawatomies and Ottawas were in
the habit of hunting buffalo west of the river,
which gave offense to the Illinoians, the owners
of the country, and who regarded these hunting
parties as trespassers on their rights.

A party of about thirty Ottawa hunters, among
whom was Pontiac, had been killing buffalo during the day on the prairie, about eight leagues
west of La Vantum.   At night they camped in a
grove of timber, with the intention of renewing

the hunt the following day. Next morning, while this hunting party were sitting around the camp-fire cooking their breakfast, unconscious of danger, they were attacked by a large party of Illinois warriors, and the most of them slain. Pontiac was wounded in this affair, but by the swiftness of his pony made his escape.*

A bloody war followed this massacre of the hunting party, and for a long time was carried on with varying success, both sides meeting with victories and defeats. The Pottawatomies and Ottawas would send war parties into the Illinois

---

*The grove referred to is supposed to have been the head of Bureau timber, near the village of La Moille, and known in the early settlement of the country as Dimmick Grove. In the spring of 1830 Daniel Dimmick made a claim here, and built a cabin near the head of the grove, on what is now known as the Collin's farm. He lived on this claim about two years, until the beginning of the Black Hawk war, when he left it and never returned, but for many years the grove bore his name.

A short distance below Dimmick's cabin, near the bank of Pike creek, and by the side of a spring, was an old Indian camping ground, and during the fall and winter hunting parties were frequently found here. In the winter of 1830-31, a party of Indians from the Illinois river, among whom was the noted chief Shick Shack, were encamped here for many days, while hunting deer in the grove.

Shick Shack said to Dimmick, while in conversation, that a long time ago a hunting party of Ottawa Indians were encamped on this very spot, when they were attacked by the Illinoians, a large portion of them killed, and their great war chief, Pontiac, wounded. From that time, continued the old chief, the tribes were at war with each other, which continued until all the Illinoians were slain, the last of whom perished on Starved Rock.

country, burn their towns, destroy their corn, kill their squaws and pappooses, and carry off with them ponies, furs and other valuables. Then the Illinoians would retaliate on their enemies by making raids into their country, killing, burning and destroying everything that lay in their way. After this war had continued for some time, the Illinoians sued for peace, and a council was called to agree·on terms.

INDIAN COUNCIL—PONTIAC ASSASSINATED.

The council met at a mound near the present site of Joliet, and was attended by all the war-chiefs of the respective tribes. For a time, the deliberations of the council were harmonious, but when the allies claimed a part of the Illinois territory as the only condition of peace, there arose an ill feeling among them. Kineboo, the head chief of the Illinoians, in a speech, said: "Rather than submit to these terms, he and his warriors would sacrifice the last drop of blood in their veins, and leave their squaws and pappooses to be scalped by a barbarous enemy." Pontiac next addressed the council. His tall, manly form, unimpaired by age, was an object of admiration, and his sprightly eloquence carried all his friends with him. With great enthusiasm he called on his brother chiefs to stand by him, and never lay down the tomahawk until their terms were acceded to. While Pontiac was thus talking, Kinéboo drew his scalping knife and stabbed him to the heart. Thus perished the greatest warrior of his day.

History gives various accounts of Pontiac's death, the year and place of its occurrence, and the manner of his end are conflicting. One account says he was assassinated in council; another that he was killed in a drunken row at Cahokia, and also killed while on a buffalo hunt. However, all accounts agree that in avenging his death a war was inaugurated which resulted in the annihilation of the Illinois Indians, but all fail to show any connection between the two events.*

*In the summer of 1767 a large, prepossessing Ottawa Indian, dressed in a French uniform, with a white feather in his cap, came to St. Louis and represented himself to the commander of the post, Lieut. Ange, as Pontiac. Some days afterward, this pompous Indian crossed the river in a canoe and went down to Cahokia, where he was much lionized by French and half-breeds, all of whom believed him to be the great Ottawa chief, Pontiac. Indians from a neighboring village came in to see him and listen to his boasting harangues, in which he said he intended to unite all the tribes of the west, drive the British from the country, and restore to the French all their former trading posts.

An English trader at Cahokia, named Williamson, being afraid that Pontiac would induce his new made friends to destroy his stock in trade, gave a drunken Indian a barrel of whisky to assassinate him. While the reputed Pontiac was sitting on the ground at the root of a tree, explaining to those

The assassination of Pontiac caused mourning throughout the country, and preparations were made to avenge his death. Runners were sent among the Winnebagoes of the north, and among the Kickapoos of the southeast, all of whom agreed to take part in the war and punish the murderers of this great Indian champion.

With these tribes united, the war was renewed with great vigor, and for savage barbarity it has no parallel in Indian warfare. Instead of its being a war of conquest, as before, it became a war of extermination, and resulted in the annihilation of the Illinois Indians, and their country occupied by the conquerors, as will be shown in the succeeding chapters.

Over the remains of Pontiac the warriors held a council, at which they swore by the great

around him the plans which he had adopted to drive the red coats out of the country, the drunken Indian employed by Williamson came up behind him and buried his tomahawk in his brain. An account of this affair found its way into the newspapers of the day, and became a matter of history. This account of the death of Pontiac was strengthened by his actual death, which occurred a year or two afterward, and explains to some extent the errors of history.

According to the statement of Shaubena, Waubonsie, and other Indians, Pontiac was assassinated while speaking in council at Mt. Joliet, and the war which followed it caused the destruction of the Illinois Indians.

A band of Ottawa Indians, known as Pontiac's, were living at a village on Kankakee river, in the early settlement of the country, and their descendants are now living in Western Kansas.

Manito of war that the fallen champion's death should be avenged, and they set to work preparing for its execution. As soon as Pontiac had breathed his last, they cut off his head and legs, boiled them to separate the flesh from the bones, and with the skull and cross-bones placed on a pointed pole, were prepared to go forth to victory.

Warriors of different tribes, who had fought with Pontiac against the British, now came forward to avenge his death. Pottawatamies, of Michigan, Miamis and Kickapoos, from the Wabash, came west and took part in the war. Even the white outlaw, Bernett, who had long since become a savage and a chief of a small band, marshaled his warriors and took part in the bloody strife which followed. The combined forces of the different tribes constituted the most formidable Indian army ever collected in the west, and for savage brutality their acts have no parallel in the history of Indian warfare. Their motto was victory or death—no quarter to the enemy, and never lay down the tomahawk until the Illinoians were annihilated.

The allied forces attacked and destroyed all the villages along the Illinois river, killing and scalping defenceless squaws and pappooses; but the principal town, La Vantum, which was well fortified and defended by the bravest warriors, they had not molested. At this town the remnants of the different bands were collected, and here they intended to make their last defense against the victorious invaders.

Small timbers and brush were brought from the neighboring groves, with which barricades were erected around three sides of the town, the river bounding the fourth. Inside this fortification were collected, from many distant towns, all that was now left of the Illinois Indians, numbering about ten thousand, of whom two thousand were warriors.

Days and weeks passed away—the summer was almost ended—and the enemy had not been seen in the vicinity, so they came to the conclusion that they had left the country. Preparations were made for holding a great feast and offering up sacrifices to the Manito of war for deliverance from the tomahawks, and scalping knives of their enemies. Fronting the council-house an altar was erected, and many of their most valuable articles burned thereon. A number of favorite dogs were killed and roasted whole, on which the warriors feasted, while offering up prayer and thanksgiving to the gods of war. Music and dancing was again heard in the great Illinois capital, and the people, old and young, gave themselves up to enjoyment. The warriors

brought forth the scalps taken from the enemy,
and in merry glee danced around them. Naked
pappooses played in the dirt, and ran to and fro
yelling and laughing as in former times. Young
maidens and their lovers amused themselves with
songs and dances, and talked of happy days in
future. For weeks the Indians gave themselves
up to feasting and amusement, unconscious of the
great calamity which was about to befall them.

It was near the close of a warm day in the
early part of Indian summer, when the Indians
of both sexes, arrayed in their best apparel, ornamented with beads, feathers and rings, were
collected in an open square on the river bank to
celebrate the marriage of the head chief's daughter.
But while in the midst of gaity, they were horrified to see the great meadow back of the town,
covered with the enemy, who, with great rapidity,
were moving on them. In front of the invaders,
on a red pole, was carried the skull and cross-
bones of Pontiac, showing that no quarter would
be asked or given.

The drums beat; the warriors grasped their
arms, and in a moment were ready for battle,
while a wail of lamentation was raised by the
frightened squaws and pappooses. On came the
allied forces, with their war-clubs and tomahawks
raised above their heads, and so rapid was their

movement, without opposition, a large number of them scaled the breastwork and entered the town. But here the assailants were met by the defenders, and most of them slain before they could recross it and join their comrades. When the invaders saw the fate of their advanced force, they were spell-bound, and before recovering from their panic, the Illinoians in a large force attacked them, when they fled in confusion, leaving behind their dead and wounded.

The attacking party being repulsed with great slaughter, retired to Buffalo Rock, where they called a council of war, at which speeches were made by the leading war-chiefs, all of whom favored prosecuting the war.

In this council it was agreed to renew the attack in the morning, and never cease fighting until the Illinoians were exterminated. The morning came, and with it came blood and carnage, unequaled in Indian warfare.

After the invaders were repulsed the Illinoians spent the night in dancing over the scalps they had taken during the day, and offering up sacrifices to the great Manito of war for their success in battle. Having spent the night in rejoicing they were found asleep in the morning, and while in this situation were again attacked, and before they could marshal their hosts the invaders, in great numbers, entered the town, killing all that lay in their course, sparing neither squaws, pappooses, aged or infirm. But the assailants were again met by brave Illinois warriors and repulsed with great slaughter. Again and again the town was entered, when a hand to hand conflict raged with fearful strife, the allies falling back only for reinforcements.

For twelve long hours the battle raged, a large portion of the Illinois warriors were slain, and hundreds of squaws and pappooses lay lifeless in their bloody gore. Night at last came, but the battle continued, and against the large invading force the defenders could make but a feeble resistance, and soon all must be slain. But fortunately a heavy rain storm came on, and in the darkness of the night it became impossible to distinguish friends from foes, consequently further slaughter was suspended until morning.

CHAPTER XIV.

THE ROCK OF REFUGE.[*]

During a heavy rain storm and the darkness of the night, the Illinoians launched their canoes, crossed the river and ascended Starved Rock. Here on this rock were collected the remnant of the Illinois Indians, consisting of about twelve hundred, three hundred of whom were warriors. On this rock the fugitives considered themselves safe from their enemies, and they offered up prayers and sang songs of praise to the great Manito for their safe deliverance. Many years

---

[*] On the 16th of September, 1873, a meeting was held on Starved Rock to commemorate the two hundredth anniversary of its discovery by Joliet and Marquette. This meeting was attended by a large number of people from the neighboring towns, many speeches were made, toasts given, and the celebration was a great success. A high pole was erected on the summit of the Rock from which waved the stars and stripes, where the French flag had waved nearly two centuries before.

At this meeting, one Perry Armstrong of Grundy county, delivered a speech entitled, "A Legend of Starved Rock," purporting to be the statement of an old Indian chief named Shick Shack. This speech was extensively copied by news-before, Tonti, with fifty French soldiers and one hundred Indian allies, held this rock when attacked by two thousand Iroquois, and put them to flight; consequently, on this spot they felt secure.

Morning came, and with it a clear sky and a bright sun; and from their elevated position they looked down on their enemies encamped on the great meadow below. Soon the allied forces were in motion, moving on the town for the purpose of completing their bloody work; but they soon discovered that their intended victims had fled. The town was burned and the slain left unburied, where their swollen and distorted remains were found some days afterwards.

papers, and read with interest by those who regarded the legend quite probable, if not strictly true.

Poor old Shick Shack, who long since had gone to the happy hunting grounds of his fathers, was made to give a detailed account of many great battles fought along the Illinois river, and the final tragedy on Starved Rock, in all of which he bore a part, but in fact must have occurred a short time before he was born, if we credit the traditions of others.

But the most remarkable part of Shick Shack's story, is the great duel fought near Terre Haute, Indiana, with three hundred on a side and among the combatants was himself and another chief named Sugar. This duel lasted twelve long hours, when all the warriors were killed except five on one side and seven on the other. The old chief informed us that neither himself nor Sugar were killed in this long and bloody affair.

This great duel described by Shick Shack, is thought to be the same one spoken of in the Bible between the hosts of Abner and Joab, and the place of meeting, Pool of Gibeon, instead of Terre Haute, as above stated, and the number of combatants having been increased from twelve on each side to three hundred, in order to correspond with the balance of the legend.

The allied forces forded the river on the rapids, surrounded Starved Rock, and prepared themselves for ascending it in order to complete their victory. With deafening yells the warriors crowded up the rocky pathway, but on reaching the summit they were met by brave Illinoians, who, with war-clubs and tomahawks, sent them bleeding and lifeless down the rugged precipice. Others ascended the rock to take part in the fight, but they, too, met the fate of their comrades. Again and again the assailants rallied, and rushed forward to assist their friends, but one after another were slain on reaching its summit, and their lifeless bodies thrown from the rock into the river. On came fresh bands of assailants, who were made valiant by their late victory, and the fearful struggle continued until the rock was red and slippery with human gore. After losing many of their bravest warriors, the attacking forces abandoned the assault and retired from the bloody scene.

Connected with this bloody battle on Starved Rock is a romantic story, which was current at the time among the French and half-breeds at Peoria, and is now told by their descendants. A young warrior, named Belix, a half-breed, who had distinguished himself in previous battles, and therefore wore on his breast a badge of honor.

This young brave having wooed and won a beautiful maiden, a daughter of the head chief, Kineboo, and the time had arrived to celebrate the marriage rites. But in the midst of the marriage festival, and before the bride was given away, the alarm of an approaching enemy was given, as previously stated. When the allied forces assaulted the fugitives on Starved Rock, foremost among the warriors in repelling the assailants, was Belix, and with his war-club cleaved the skulls of many of the enemy. During the fight his fancied bride stood near by witnessing the bloody strife, but when she saw her lover's skull split open by a tomahawk, with a wild scream she sprang from the rock down the fearful precipice, her body falling from crag to crag, until it landed lifeless and bleeding in the river below.

THE BESIEGERS AND BESIEGED.

On a high, rocky cliff south of Starved Rock, and known as Devil's Nose, the allied forces erected a temporary fortification. During the night they collected small timbers and evergreen brush, with which they erected a breastwork. From this breastwork they fired on the besieged, killing some and wounding others, among the latter was Kineboo, the head chief of the tribe.

The fortifications protecting the south part of
Starved Rock, had fallen into decay, fifty-one
years having elapsed since the French abandoned
Fort St. Louis. The palisades had rotted off, and
the earthworks mouldered away to one-half their
original hight, consequently they afforded but little
protection. To remedy the defect on this side of
the old fortress, the besieged cut down some of
the stunted cedars that crowded the summit of
the rock, with which they erected barricades along
the embankment to shield themselves from the
arrows and rifle balls of the enemy.

The besieged were now protected from the
missiles of their assailants, but another enemy
equally dreaded—that of hunger and thirst—be-
gan to alarm them. When they took refuge here
on the rock, they carried with them a quantity of
provisions, but this supply was now exhausted
and starvation stared them in the face. At
first this rock was thought to be a haven of
safety, but now it was likely to be their tomb,
and without a murmur brave warriors made
preparations to meet their fate. Day after day
passed away, mornings and evenings came and
went, and still the Illinoians continued to be
closely guarded by the enemy, leaving them no
opportunity to escape from their rocky prison.

Famishing with thirst caused them to cut up

some of their buckskin clothing, out of which they made cords to draw water out of the river, but the besiegers had placed a guard at the base of the rock, and as soon as the vessel reached the water they would cut the cord, or by giving it a quick jerk the water drawer would be drawn over the precipice, and his body fall lifeless into the river.

As days passed away, the besieged sat on the rock, gazing on the great meadow below, over which they had oftimes roamed at pleasure, and they sighed for freedom once more. The site of their town was in plain view, but instead of lodges and camping tents, with people passing to and fro, as in former days, it was now a lonely, dismal waste, blackened by fire and covered with the swollen and ghastly remains of the slain. Buzzards were hovering around, flying back and forth over the desolated town, and feasting on the dead bodies of their friends.

At night they looked upon the silent stars toward the spirit land, and in their wild imagination saw angels waiting to receive them. While sleeping they dreamed of roaming over woods and prairie in pursuit of game, or cantering their ponies across the plains, but on awakening it was found all a delusion. Their sleep was disturbed by the moans and sighs of the suffering, and

when morning came it was but the harbinger of
another day of torture. From their rocky prison
they could see the ripe corn in their fields, and
on the distant prairie a herd of buffalo were graz-
ing, but while in sight of plenty they were famishing for food. Below them, at the base of the
rock, flowed the river, and as its rippling waters
glided softly by, it appeared in mockery to their
burning thirst.

They had been twelve days on the rock, closely
guarded by the enemy, much of the time suffering from hunger and thirst. Their small stock
of provision was long since exhausted, and early
and late the little ones were heard crying for
food. The mother would hold her infant to her
breast, but alas the fountain that supported life
had dried up, and the little sufferer would turn
its head away with a feeble cry. Young maidens,
whose comely form, sparkling eyes and blooming
cheeks were the pride of their tribe, became
pale, feeble and emaciated, and with a feeling of
resignation they looked upward to their home in
the spirit land. One of the squaws, the wife of
a noted chief, while suffering in a fit of delirium
caused by hunger and thirst, threw her infant
from the summit of the rock into the river below,
and with a wild, piercing scream, followed it.

A few brave warriors attempted to escape from

their prison, but on descending from the rock were slain by the vigilant guards. Others in their wild frenzy hurled their tomahawks at the fiends below, and singing their death song, laid down to die.

The last lingering hope was now abandoned; hunger and thirst had done its dreadful work; the cries of the young and lamentations of the aged were heard only in a whisper; their tongues swollen and their lips crisped from thirst so they could scarcely give utterance to their sufferings. Old white headed chiefs, feeble and emaciated, being reduced almost to skeletons, crept away under the branches of evergreens and breathed their last. Proud young warriors preferred to die upon this strange rocky fortress by starvation and thirst, rather than surrender themselves to the scalping knives of a victorious enemy. Many had died; their remains were lying here and there on the rock, and the effluvium caused by putrefaction greatly annoyed the besiegers. A few of the more hardy warriors for a time feasted on the dead, eating the flesh and drinking the blood of their comrades as soon as life was extinct.

A party of the allied forces now ascended the rock and tomahawked all those who had survived the famine. They scalped old and young, and left the remains to decay on the rock, where their bones were seen many years afterward.

Thus perished the large tribe of Illinois Indians, and with the exception of a solitary warrior, they became extinct.

Near the close of the siege of starved Rock, a young warrior, during a severe storm and darkness of the night, took a buckskin cord which had been used for drawing water, and fastening it to the trunk of a tree let himself down into the river. Escaping detection by the guards, he swam down the river and thus secured his liberty, being the only survivor of this fearful tragedy. This warrior was partly white, being a descendant on his father's side from the French, who settled around Fort St. Louis many years before. Being alone in the world, without kindred or friends, he went to Peoria, joined the colony, and there ended his days. He embraced Christianity, became an officer in the church, and was christened under an old French name, La Bell. His descendants are now living near Prairie du Rocher, one of whom, Charles La Bell, was a party to a suit in the United States Court to recover the land where the city of Peoria now stands *

* In the early settlement of the country there was an old Indian named Meachelle, who frequently visited the trading posts at Hennepin and Ottawa, and made various statements about the Starved Rock tragedy. He said he was a boy at the time, accompanying his father; was present and saw the destruction

A GHASTLY SPECTACLE.

A few days after the destruction of the Illinois
Indians, a party of traders from Peoria, among
whom were Robert Maillet and Felix La Pance,
while on their return from Canada with three
canoes loaded with goods, stopped at the scene of
the late tragedy. As they approached Starved
Rock, which at that time was called Le Rocher,
they noticed a cloud of buzzards hovering over
it, and at the same time they were greeted with a
sickening odor. On landing from their canoes
and ascending the rock, they found the steep,
rocky pathway leading thereto stained with blood,

of the last of the Illinois Indians. After many days siege, said
he, a large number of warriors descended from the rock and
made an attempt to fight their way through the lines, but were
all slain except seven, who succeeded in escaping down the
river to Peoria, and found refuge among the French.

As late as the year 1828, a small band of Indians lived on Lake
Dupue, and raised corn on a little bottom prairie, now included
in a farm owned by Charles Savage. Among these Indians was
a very old man, who frequently accompanied his grandson in a
canoe to Hartzell's trading house. This old man said that he
was born on the Wabash, and was ten years old at the time of
the Starved Rock tragedy. His father participated in this
affair, and two of his uncles were killed in the fight with the
Illinoians before they took refuge on Starved Rock. He said
the fight continued for two days at the town, and hundreds of
warriors on both sides were slain, but during a rain storm and
darkness of the night, the remnant of the Illinoians escaped to
Starved Rock.

Two years after this affair, the band to which the old Indian
belonged emigrated to Illinois, and built a town on the south
side of the river, opposite Lake Dupue. At that time, and for

and among the stunted cedars that grew on the cliff were lodged many human bodies, partly devoured by birds of prey. But on reaching the summit of Le Rocher, they were horrified to find it covered with dead bodies, all in an advanced state of decomposition. Here were aged chiefs, with silvered locks, lying by the side of young warriors, whose long raven black hair partly concealed their ghastly and distorted features. Here, too, were squaws and pappooses, the aged grandmother and the young maiden, with here and there an infant, still clasped in its mother's arms.

many years afterwards, the summit of the rock was covered with bones and skulls. Two miles below Starved Rock, on the site of the town, where a great battle was fought, many acres of ground were covered with human bones.

An old Indian called Shaddy, who went west with his band in 1834, but afterwards returned to look once more upon the scene of his youth, and hunted on Bureau and along the Illinois river in the winter of 1836. From this old Indian I gathered many items in relation to past events. He said that his father was at the siege of Starved Rock, and all the Illinois Indians perished except one. This was a young half-breed, who let himself down into the river by means of a buckskin cord, during a severe rain storm, and in the darkness of the night made his escape.

According to history, about one thousand Illinoians, but known as Kaskaskia Indians, were living in the south part of the State as late as 1802. The Indians at the south appear to have taken no part in the war, and the destruction of the tribe applied only to those along the Illinois river.

It is said some of the Illinois tribe took refuge with the French at Peoria, and were afterwards known as Peoria Indians.

These conflicting statements are given only for what they are worth, and from which the reader can draw his own conclusions.

Some had died from thirst and starvation, others by the tomahawk or war-club; of the latter a pool of clotted blood was seen at their side. All the dead, without regard to age or sex, had been scalped, and their remains, divested of clothing, were lying here and there on the rock. These swollen and distorted remains were hideous to look upon, and the stench from them so offensive that the traders hastened down from the rock and continued on their way down the river.

On reaching La Vantum, a short distance below Le Rocher, the traders met with a still greater surprise, and for a time were almost ready to believe what they saw was all delusion instead of a reality. The great town of the west had disappeared; not a lodge, camping tent, nor one human being could be seen; all was desolate, silent and lonely. The ground where the town had stood was strewn with dead bodies, and a pack of hungry wolves were feeding upon their hideous repast.

Five months before, these traders, while on their way to Canada, stopped at La Vantum for a number of days in order to trade with the Indians. At that time the inhabitants of the town —about five thousand in number—were in full enjoyment of life, but now their dead bodies lay mouldering on the ground, food for wolves and

buzzards.   Maillet and La Pance had bought of
these people two canoe loads of furs and pelts,
which were to be paid in goods on their return
from Canada.   The goods were now here to make
payment, according to contract, but alas the cred-
itors had all gone to their long home.

The smell from hundreds of putrified and partly
consumed remains, was so offensive that the
traders remained only a short time, and with
sadness they turned away from this scene of horror.   Again boarding their canoes they passed
down the river to Peoria, conveying thither to
their friends the sad tidings.

RELICS OF THE TRAGEDY.

On the following spring, after the annihilation
of the Illinoians Indians, a party of traders from
Cahokia, in canoes loaded with furs, visited Canada, making thither their annual trip in accordance with their former custom.   On reaching
Peoria they heard of the destruction of the Illinois Indians on Starved Rock, and were afraid to
proceed further on their journey, not knowing
but the victors were still in the country, and they,
too, would meet with a like fate.   After remaining a few days at Peoria, they proceeded on their
way, accompanied (as far as Starved Rock) by

twenty armed Frenchmen and about thirty Indian. With this escort was Father Jacques Buche,
a Jesuit priest of Peoria, and some account of his
observations are preserved in his mauscript.*

When the voyageurs arrived at LaVantum, they
found the town site strewn with human bones.
These, with a few charred poles, alone marked
the location of the former great town of the west.
Scattered over the prairie were hundreds of skulls.
Some of these retained a portion of flesh and were
partly covered with long black hair, giving to the
remains a ghastly and sickening appearance.

This party also ascended Le Rocher, and found
its summit covered with bones and skulls. Among
these were found knives, tomahawks, rings,
beads and various trinkets, some of which the
travelers carried with them to Canada, and now
can be seen among the antiquarian collection at
Quebec.

Various accounts are given, both by French
and Indians, of seeing in after years relics of this
tragical affair on the summit of Starved Rock.
Bulbona, a French Indian trader, who was known
by many of the early settlers, said when a
small boy he accompanied his father in ascending
Starved Rock, and there saw many relics

*An account of this manuscript will be found in the succeed-
ing chapter, and from which many extracts are taken.

of this fearful tragedy. This was only fifteen years after the massacre of the Illinois Indians, and the rock was covered with skulls and bones, all in a good state of preservation, but bleached white by rain and sun.

On my first visit to Starved Rock, nearly forty years ago, I found a number of human teeth and small fragments of bones. Others have found relics of the past, such as beads, rings, knives, &c.

About thirty-five years ago a human skull, partly decayed, was found at the root of a cedar tree, buried up with leaves and dirt. A rusty tomahawk and a large scalping knife, with other articles, also human bones, were taken out of a pit hole, a few years ago. The early settlers have found many things on the summit of Starved Rock, and still retain them in their possession as relics of the past.

CHAPTER XV.

In the river timber, about one-half mile south-east of Starved Rock, and on land belonging to Mrs. Gabet, is still to be seen the remains of an ancient fortification. This work of antiquity is located on a level piece of ground, at the inter-section of two ravines, and consists of low, irregu-lar earthworks. These earthworks follow the course of the ravines on two sides, forming zig-zag lines, with an open gateway at the east, front-ing the prairie. These lines enclose about one acre of ground, of an oblong shape, and is now covered with large trees. This old relic appears to have been only a temporary fortification, con-sisting of a ditch, an embankment, and perhaps palisades. At what time this fortification was erected, by whom and for what purpose, will probably remain a mystery.

There are various opinions about these old earthworks. Some believe they were erected by the French while in possession of Fort St. Louis, and intended as a summer fort to protect themselves from the Indians while raising a crop on the adjoining prairie. But this is not probable, as the prairie near by, in the early settlement of the country, showed no marks of ever having been cultivated; and protection from the Indians was unnecessary, as they always lived on friendly terms with them. It could not have been the work of the French, for it shows no signs of civil engineering, and neither history nor tradition give any account of it.

A few years ago a large burr oak was cut within the fortification, and near the heart of it was found imbedded a rifle ball, which, according to the growths, must have been put there more than a century ago. There are a number of large trees growing on the embankment and in the ditch, on various parts of the fortification, which is evidence of its great antiquity. This old relic is, without doubt, a work of the Mound Builders, as similar remains are found elsewhere.

About two hundred yards northeast of this old fort, by the side of a small ravine, a coal bank was recently opened by James Bain, but on account of the thinness of the vein it was found unprofitable to work. This vein of coal is close to the surface, only a few feet under ground, and near the place where it was opened is a large cavity in the earth. On examining this cavity or excavation, it was found that the coal had been taken out, and the enbankment on either side, caused by throwing out the dirt, are now covered with trees. This work must have been done centuries ago, and some believe by the occupants of the fort above described.

RELICS OF ANTIQUITY.

In the vicinity of Starved Rock many relics of the early French explorers have been found, consisting of farming implements of European manufacture, rifle and cannon balls, gold and silver crosses, two bronze medallion heads, one of Louis XIV, and the other Pope Leo X.

A few years ago a small cannon was found near Ottawa, imbedded in the river bank, where, in all probability, it had remained a century or more. This cannon is constructed of wrought iron, hooped with heavy rings to give it strength, like those used in Europe three hundred years ago. This ancient piece of ordnance, in all probability, was brought from Canada in a canoe by La Salle, or some of his men, to be used on a fortification. It may have been the first one mounted on the ramparts of Fort St. Louis, and at the time of its dedication fired a salute in honor of the king of France.

A short time ago an old cedar tree was cut on the summit of Starved Rock, and within its trunk was found imbedded a gun-barrel, partly destroyed by rust. How this gun-barrel came here will forever remain a mystery, but in all probability it was the work of an ingenious Frenchman during the occupation of Fort St. Louis. This gun-barrel, with a portion of the tree which surrounded it, are preserved among the collections of relics in Ottawa.

A few months ago, David Walker found near Buffalo Rock a piece of copper, about the size and shape of a half dollar. This curious relic is carved with rude characters, among which can be traced the name of Tonti. It is quite probable this is one of the medals which the commander of Fort St. Louis distributed among his Indian friends, of which we have an account.

While digging a cellar for a house, near the base of Starved Rock, a short time ago, a human skull was found, in which was a large sized flint arrow head. On one side of the forehead of this skull is a hole where the missile of death had entered. This skull, arrow head, Tonti's medal, an iron Indian ax, on which is the name of Standish, with a large collection of other Indian relics, are now in the possession of David Walker of Ottawa.

Near Starved Rock, on both sides of the river, many Indian relics have been found, consisting of gun flints arrow heads, earthen pots and kettles, with tomahawks, knives, hoes, &c., made of stone. Many of these relics have been collected by people living in that locality, and will be preserved in "The Ottawa Academy of Natural Science."

On the north side of the river, a short distance above Starved Rock, and on the bottom prairie, are three sulphur springs. One of these springs is very large, boiling up among the white sand, and throwing out a large volume of clear water strongly impregnated with saline matter. In former times Indians from different parts of the country, afflicted with maladies, came here for medical treatment, which to some extent accounts for the great amount of relics found in this vicinity.*

LOUISIANA COLONY.

This colony as has been previously stated, was founded by La Salle, at Fort St. Louis, in the year

*In the year 1853 a large stone house, called the Sulphur Spring Hotel, was built here with the expectation of making this a great watering place, but the enterprise was a failure. Notwithstanding the extensive advertising by those interested, hey did not succeed in making it a Saratoga nor a Homburg.

1682, under a charter from the king of France, and was called Louisiana in honor of Louis XIV. The colony existed here until 1718, a period of thirty-six years, but had it continued permanently La Salle county would have been the oldest settled place in the west. One year after this colony was established, La Salle gave Richard Bosley a permit to trade with the Indians at Cahokia, where Father Allonez had previously established a mission. Emigrants from Canada came to Cahokia, many of whom became permanent residents, and from that time people continued to reside here, therefore it now claims to be the oldest settlement in the Mississippi valley. The French erected houses in the town with the Indians, and all lived together in harmony. Marriages between the French and Indians were legalized by the Catholic church, and many of the traders found wives among the blooming daughters of Illinois. Some of the present inhabitants of Cahokia can trace their genealogy back to the time of La Salle, their ancestors having intermarried with the natives, so that in many families the Indian blood predominates.

A French settlement was soon after made at Kaskaskia, and a few years later a colony was planted on the lower Mississippi. The whole country took the name of Louisiana, designating the north and south part by Illinois and Mississippi.

The king of France gave Crozat a patent for all the Louisiana country, over which he was to have control for twenty years, for the purpose of mining and trading with the Indians. This patent bears date September 14, 1711, and was ratified by the colonists of Kaskaskia, Cahokia and Fort St. Louis. Colonel La Mott, an agent of Crozat, took possession of the country, assuming the title of Governor, and made Kaskaskia the capital. The Indians showed the new governor two pieces of silver ore, which they said were taken out of Illinois mines, but in fact came from Mexico. Thinking only of making a great fortune, the governor employed a company of miners, and went north in search of the precious metal. Lead and copper in great abundance were found, but no silver nor gold. After prospecting for two years, and expending large sums of money in searching for the precious metal, without meeting with success, the scheme was abandoned.

Crozat, after five years experience in mining and trading with the Indians, found it unprofitable, so he surrendered his patent to the French Court, and Governor La Mott, with many of the miners, returned to France.

On the year following the surrender of Crozat's

patent, a similar one was granted to George Law, a Scotch banker of Paris, and by his orders Fort Charters, on the Mississippi, was built.

In the spring of 1736 D. Arquette commander in Illinois, and Captain Vincennes, of a trading post on the Wabash, (which still bears his name), with about one hundred French soldiers and many Indian allies, went to lower Louisiana to assist Governor Bieneville in prosecuting a war against the Chickasaws. This expedition proved a failure, and the two commanders and Father Senac, with many of the soldiers, were taken prisoners and burned at the stake. While the flames enveloped their bodies, Father Senac, amid the blazing faggots, exhorted his companions to die as become Frenchmen and Christians, and while racked with torture he administered to his dying countrymen the last rites of the Catholic church.

The colony in Illinois continued under French rule until 1765, when it became subject to Great Britain, and afterwards to the United States.

THE BUFFALO.

The flesh of the buffalo furnished the Indians with food, their skins with clothing, bedding and tents ; their sinews for bows, the bones and horns for ornaments ; consequently, when these animals

left the country, the wild savages of the west
were deprived of many of the comforts of life.

According to the statement of the early French
explorers, and also confirmed by Indian traditions, the country west of the great bend in the
Illinois river, was the great buffalo range, and
here their bones were found in large quantities
in the early settlement of the country.

At what time the buffalo left the country is
not known, but in comparing the various statements of traders and Indians, it must have been
between 1780 and 7190.   In the year 1778, An-
tonine Des Champs, then a lad of eight years of
age, came with his parents from Canada to Peoria, and lived there until the town was destroyed,
thirty-four years afterwards.   Des Champs said,
for some years after he came to Peoria, buffalo
were plenty, and he had frequently seen large
herds of them swimming the Illlnois river.   Previous to 1790 the French had an extensive trade
in buffalo robes, but after that period there were
none shipped from the Illinois river.

In the early settlement of the country, old Indians were living here who said in their youthful
days they had seen large herds of buffalo on the
prairies, but they all perished in a big snow,
which covered the ground many feet in depth,
and crusted over so a person could walk on it.

Next spring a few buffalo, poor and haggard in appearance, were seen going westward, and as they approached the carcasses of the dead buffalo, which were lying on the prairie in great numbers, they would stop, commence pawing and lowing, and then start off again on a lope for the west, and from that time buffalo were seldom seen east of the Mississippi river.

Although the buffalo had left the country, as above stated, a few stray ones were occasionally seen here in after years, and as late as 1815, the Indians attacked a herd between the Illinois and Green rivers, killing two of them.

Forty years ago buffalo bones were plenty on the prairies; and in three different places in Bureau county many acres of ground were covered with them, showing where large herds had perished. Skulls of buffalo, with horns still on them, were frequently found here, and their trails leading to and from watering places were plain to be seen, in the early settlement of the country.*

PAT KENNEDY'S JOURNAL.

Through the politeness of Lyman C. Draper, Secretary of the Wisconsin Historical Society, and author of a number of historical collections, I have been furnished with a manuscript copy of

*Reminiscences of Bureau County,

Patrick Kennedy's journal, of his travels up the Illinois river, and from which the following items are gathered :

On the 23, of July, 1773, Kennedy, with a party of adventurers, left Kaskaskia in a keel-boat, and ascended the river in search of copper mines. On arriving at the foot of the rapids they left their boat and proceeded up the river on foot, forty-five miles. Here on an island they found encamped a party of French traders, but failing to obtain any information of them in relation to the copper mines, they abandoned the search and returned to Kaskaskia.

Kennedy's journal speaks of seeing large herds of buffalo, elk and deer, feeding on the big meadow on both sides of the river. It also gives an account of a saline spring and lake, where the French and Indians were engaged in making salt. It refers to a cliff of rocks not far from the mouth of Fox river, where the French obtained their mill-stones.

This journal gives a geographical description of the country—size and names of rivers, and a general account of the Illinois region, but throws no light on the history of the French settlements. It refers to the town and fort at Peoria Lake, but says nothing of the size of the place, of its inhabitants or general appearance.

This old manuscript is now in the hands of Hypolite Pilette, who lives on the American Bottom, between Cahokia and Prairie du Rocher. It consists of twenty-three pages, closely written, on large sheets, and from age the paper is yellow and ink faded. This manuscript is in the French language, dated La Ville de Maillet (now Peoria), A. D. 1770, and was written by Jacques Buche, a Catholic priest.

The writer speaks only of things that came under his own observation, and relates many remarkable incidents which are worth preserving. Some of these statements differ from the traditions of others, but nevertheless are not improbable, as they carry with them an air of truth.

Father Buche's manuscript forms a connecting link of history between the time of La Salle and the destruction of Peoria, and from its pages many of the incidents narrated in this book have been taken. It speaks of the destruction of La Vantum, and the perishing of the remnant of the Illinois Indians on Starved Rock.

It also gives an account of digging for gold within the stockades of Fort St. Louis, the pit-holes of which are now plain to be seen.

Father Buche speaks of visiting an Indian village, fifteen leagues north of Peoria, where he remained

many day, teaching the people the ways of Christianity. The inhabitants of this village, said he,
were possessed of the devil, indulging in vile
practices and idolatrous worship. The chiefs had
many wives, and put them to death if they proved
barren. At their religious feast, which took place
once a year, an infant of some noted chief was
burned on the altar as a sacrifice to the great
Manito. This was done in order that the band
might be successful in war, hunting and fishing,
and also to protect them from the power of the
evil one.

Father Buche said he preached many times to
these benighted people, and the chiefs and
many warriors were converted to Christianity.
In one day he baptized about fifty persons, whose
names were enrolled in the church book, and their
souls saved from perdition.

THE GREAT BUFFALO HUNT.

In Father Buche's manuscript, is an account of
a great buffalo hunt, which took place on the
prairie west of the Iliinois river. He says that
he accompanied thirty-eight of his countrymen
and about three hundred Indians on a buffalo
hunt, when they killed so many that their hides
alone were taken, and their carcasses left on the

prairie, food for wolves. A few leagues west of the great bend in the Illinois river, they discovered a herd of many thousand buffalo feeding on a small prairie, partly surrounded by thick timber. It being about sundown, the hunters encamped for the night in a grove near by, with the intention of attacking the herd on the following morning. Next morning before it was light, the Indians, divested of clothing, mounted on ponies and armed with guns, bows and arrows, spears, &c., were anxiously awaiting the command of their chief to commence the sport. The Indians formed a circle around the herd, secreting themselves in the timber, while the French completed a line across the prairie. The buffalo were lying thick over the prairie, chewing their cud, unconscious of approaching danger. At a given signal from the chief, the lines closed in all sides, but as soon as the animals got wind of the approaching enemy, arose to their feet and fled in great confusion. But on approaching the line the Indians fired on them, at the same time yelling at the top of their voice. The frightened creatures turned and fled in the opposite direction, where they were met by the French hunters and foiled in a like manner. Thus they continued to run back and forth from one side of the ring to the other, while the slaughter went on.

As the buffalo approached the line, the Indians would pierce their hearts with spears, or bring them down with arrows or rifle balls. The line continued to close in, and the frightened buffalo, snorting and with wild flashing eyes, would charge the guards, first on one side, then on the other, but met the missiles of death everywhere. After surging back and forth in wild confusion, the buffalo broke through the line, bearing down the guards, jumping over the prostrated ponies and their riders, and thus made their escape.

Father Buche says in his manuscript: "By the wild surging herd my pony was knocked down, and I lay prostrated by its side, while the frightened buffalo, with loud snorting and wild flashing eyes, in their flight jumped over me ; but through the protection of the Holy Virgin I was saved from instant death."

CHAPTER XVI.

JEAN BAPTISTE AND FATHER BONNER.

In the year 1790 there lived near Lexington, Kentucky, a young slave named Jean Baptiste, who was brought by his master from Virginia into that new country. Baptiste associated much with the Indians, learned their language, and became fascinated with their free, independent mode of living. His proud spirit could not be subdued by the whip of his master; therefore he severed the bond which made him a slave, and taking the north star for a guide, he soon became a free man. Armed with his master's rifle and a large hunting knife, he traveled northward about three hundred miles, through a wilderness country. On reaching Des Plaines river he found refuge in an Indian village, married a squaw and raised a family of children. One of his grandsons is now living in a hewn log house on the bank of Cahokia creek, in St. Clair county, from which I obtained the narrative relating to his distinguished grandsire.

According to the statement of Sau-ga-nash (Billy Caldwell), the first white man that settled at Chicago was a negro. This negro was no other than Jean Baptiste, above referred to, whose name is now associated with the early history of the western metropolis. He left the Indian village on Des Plains river soon after he came to the country, and built a cabin near the mouth of Chicago river, immediately north of Rush street bridge. Here he cultivated a small piece of ground, and spent much of his time in hunting and fishing, as well as concocting schemes to make himself a chief among the Indians.

Baptiste told the Indians that he had been a great chief among the whites at the south, and he expected to become one among them also. Possessing much shrewdness and a good address, this cunning negro tried various means to gain the confidence of the Indians, so that he might be proclaimed a chief among them, but all his plans failed. On account of the abundance of fish here at the mouth of the river, and the cool lake breeze in the summer made it a good place for a village, and he persuaded his Indian friends to come thither and build. He also told them that some day there would be a big town at the mouth of Chicago river, and if they occupied the land they could sell it to the whites at a good price.

His object was to build a town here on the lake shore, of which he would be the founder, and by that means become a chief. A few Indians built lodges on the north side of the river, in accordance with Baptiste's wishes, but the scattering trees afforded the village but little protection from winter storms, and the cold wind from the lake discouraged them, consequently they abandoned the lake and returned to their old village on the Des Plains.

At that time, Father Bonner, a French Jesuit priest, was living among the Indians, and for many years had been preaching to them. Baptise, being aware of the priest's influence among the Indians, thought he might use it to his own advantage, therefore he sought his friendship, and gained his confidence. He also joined the church, became a zealous Catholic, attending all meetings, making long and fervent prayers. Father Bonner thought only of making Baptiste an instrument in his hands to promote the cause of Christianity, while the unscrupulous negro expected to use the priest in advancing his claims to the chieftainship, therefore the two became intimate friends and labored for each other's interest.

Father Bonner notified all the Indians who were communicants of his church, to meet him

on St. Jerome's day at the place on Chicago river
consecrated by Father Marquette, for the purpose of offering up prayers to Christ and the
Holy Virgin, but his real object was to have
Baptiste proclaimed head chief of the band.   On
the day appointed a large number of Indians collected at the place designated, in accordance with
the priest's request, when the object of the meeting was explained to them. On the mound,
which had long been hallowed by the Indians as
the spot where Marquette built an altar, a wooden
cross was erected for the occasion.   Father Bonner, standing by the side of this cross, preached
to the Indians, and in conclusion, said that he
had a matter of great importance to lay before
them. He told them that the Holy Virgin had
visited him in a dream, and impressed upon his
mind that the advancement of Christianity required that Baptiste, by divine authority, should
be proclaimed head chief of the band.   Baptiste
now came forward and knelt by the side of the
cross, when the priest anointed him chief in the
same manner that Samuel annointed Saul, king
of Israel.   After pouring bears oil on Baptiste's
wooly head, he exclaimed in a loud voice, "By
the power and authority of the Holy Catholic
Church, I pronounce this man head chief of this
band."   When the ceremony was completed, the

priest offered up prayer in behalf of the newly appointed chief, calling on the Virgin to give him grace and wisdom in order that he might be a just and wise ruler of his people.

The Indians refused to accept Baptiste as their head chief, notwithstanding he had been appointed by high authority, and the would-be ruler returned to his cabin with a sorrowful heart. Failing to gain power over the Indians, Baptiste became disgusted with the life of a savage, abandoned his cabin and went to Peoria, where he ended his days some years afterwards.

The cabin which Baptiste built was afterwards occupied by a French trader named Le Mai, who sold it to John Kinzie in 1804, about the time Fort Dearborn was built.

Father Bonner was loved and honored by the Indians, and he remained with them until his death, which occurred one year before Fort Dearborn was built. He was not only a spiritual father, but said to be a natural one, as a number of half-breeds, known to the early settlers of Chicago, claimed to be his descendants.

PIERRE DE BEURO.

About the year 1776, a young French Creole of Cahokia, by the name of Pierre De Beuro, came to Peoria, and for a few years was employed as a clerk in a trading house. De Beuro being of an enterprising turn of mind, and well acquainted with the Indian language, left Peoria in search of his fortune. Having made the acquaintance of a number of chiefs while clerking at Peoria, he concluded to visit their villages, which were located at different points on or near the river. He stopped some time at Wappa, on Bureau creek, then at a village on Lake De Pue, and afterwards went to a large town near the mouth of Fox river. Here he married a squaw, the daughter of a noted chief, and made preparations to engage in the fur trade.

De Beuro visited Peoria to procure necessary tools for building a house, and accompanied by a half-breed he ascended the river as far as the mouth of Bureau creek, where he established a trading post.

Below the mouth of Bureau creek is an elevated piece of land, covered with timber, and known as Hickory Ridge. This place became a noted land mark with the French and Indians, and was the scene of a number of traditionary incidents. It also became a place of note in the early settlement of the country, and during high water was the landing for the Hennepin ferry-boat. Here on this ridge, elevated above the floods of the river, De Beuro, assisted by a number of Indians, built a double log cabin, and laid the foundation of a large fur trade. Being located in the heart of the Indian country, the first year he collected two canoe loads of furs and buffalo skins, which he shipped to Cahokia, and paid for them on his return with goods received in exchange.

While the traders at Peoria continued to send their furs to Canada, De Beuro sent his to Cahokia, and there obtained goods for the Indian market. Antoine Des Champs said every spring for a number of years, canoes loaded with furs and buffalo robes, passed Peoria on their way down the river from this trading house. The traders at Peoria were unfriendly toward De Beuro, as he took a large portion of their trade, and they tried to buy him out, but did not succeed. In the spring of 1790, De Beuro, in accordance with his former custom, sent two canoes loaded with furs down the river to Cahokia, in charge of his clerk and two Indians. The trader accompanied the canoes down the river about twenty miles to an Indian village for the purpose of transacting some business, and from here he started for home on foot, but never reached it. Search was made for the missing trader, and some days afterwards his remains were found a short distance from the trail, in a thick cluster of underbrush, partly devoured by wolves. He had been shot through the body, and from appearances ran a short distance when he was overtaken by the assassin and his head split open with a tomahawk.

Report says a trader at Peoria, whose descendants are now living near East St. Louis, being angry at De Beuro on account of taking away much of his trade, employed a half-breed to assassinate him, and thereby break up the rival trading post.

When the clerk found that the trader was dead, he appropriated the proceeds of the furs to his own account, and De Beuro's squaw put the goods at the trading house into canoes, and took them to her people who lived at a village near the mouth of Fox river. Thus the trading post was broken up, after being in operation fourteen years. The buildings vacated went to decay, but from this trader Bureau creek derived its name.

During the war of 1812, when the troops under General Howard, at Peoria, were preparing to ascend the river in keel boats in search of the enemy, the Indians tore down the cabins built by De Beuro, and with the logs erected a breastwork on the river bank so they could fire on the boats. But on the arrival of the boats, and finding their decks protected by heavy planking, with port holes for cannon, the Indians were stricken with panic, and fled from their breastworks without firing a gun or letting their presence be known to the troops.

Gerden S. Hubbard says, when he came to the country in 1818, this breastwork was still standing, and its relics were plain to be seen in the early settlement of the country.*

CAPTAIN LEVERING'S VISIT TO PEORIA.

In the summer of 1809, soon after Ninian Edwards was appointed Governor of Illinois territory, trouble existed between the whites and Indians, and a few persons were killed by the latter. The Indians on the Illinois river appeared shy and unfriendly, and rumors were in circulation that they meditated an attack upon the frontier settlements. These reports, and their unfriendly demonstrations, caused Governor Edwards to send Captain Levering, a native of Kaskaskia, with a small company of volunteers in a keel boat to Peoria, in order to ascertain the intention of the Indians.

Captain Levering and all his company were French Creoles, who understood the Indian

---

* A few years ago David Miller cut the timber off Hickory Ridge and put the land under cultivation. Where De Beuro's trading house stood many relics of civilization, such as pieces of pottery, glassware, &c., were plowed up.

language and customs, and with whom friendly
relation existed, even in time of war.

On arriving at Peoria the volunteers were
cordially received by both French and Indians,
who prepared for them a great feast and a ball
in the evening. Some of the guests became fascinated with the Indian maidens, two of whom
took wives home with them.

From Peoria parties were sent to different
Indian villages for the purpose of delivering presents, and have a talk with the chiefs. One of the
parties visited the Kickapoo village on Sugar
creek, about forty miles southeast of Peoria, and
the Indians here expressed a friendly feeling
towards Americans.

Joseph Trotier, a native of Cahokia, accompanied by two half-breeds, ascended the river in
a canoe as far as the great bend, stopping at
Crows, Gomo and Black Partridge's villages, and
from the chiefs and warriors received assurance
of peace and friendship. They also visited the
village of Wappa, on Bureau creek, and Comas
the head chief sent Governor Edwards as a token
of friendship, a pair of large elk horns and a
panther skin, all of which he had taken with his
own hands.

Captain Levering and company returned to
Kaskaskia, carrying with them many presents

from the chiefs to Governor Edwards, and also their pledges of friendship.

For nearly two years after Captain Levering's visit to the Indian country, the frontier settlements were not molested, but in the fall of 1811, a number of persons were killed by the Indians in Madison and St. Clair counties. At these depredations people on the frontier settlements became greatly alarmed; some fled from the country, while others built temporary forts to shield themselves from the tomahawks and scalping knives of the savages. Fort Russell was built near the present site of Edwardsville, and cannon brought from old Fort Charters and mounted on its wooden ramparts.

GOVERNOR EDWARDS MEETING THE POTTAWATO-MIE CHIEFS.

During the winter of 1811–12, the Indians at the different villages along the river, heard that preparations were being made by Governor Edwards to send an army against them in the spring. On hearing of this intended invasion by the troops, they were much alarmed, and the chiefs and principal warriors met in council at Senachwine's village, to agree on plans for the future, but no definite conclusion was arrived at. Many of the chiefs went to Peoria to consult with their friends, the French, and to procure their assistance in averting the evil which threatened them. Captain J. B. Maillet consented to go to Kaskaskia and see Governor Edwards, and pledge to him their intentions of peace and friendship. On arriving at the seat of government the Governor proposed to meet the chiefs in council at Cahokia, in the latter part of April, and there settle all misunderstandings. At the time appointed a large delegation of chiefs, among whom were Black Partridge, Senachwine and Gomo, in their canoes arrived at Cahokia.

The council was held in a little grove of timber on the bank of Cahokia creek, above the town and was attended by a large collection of people, some of whom are still living, and to them I am indebted for some facts relating to it.*

Black Partridge made a speech in the council, and while holding aloft a silver medal which he wore suspended from his neck, said : " This token

* While at Cahokia a short time ago, the place of holding this council was pointed out to me by an old man, who in his boyhood days, sixty-two years before, attended it. He described Black Partridge, Senachwine, and other chiefs, who it appears made a lasting impression upon his then youthful mind. In this little grove where the council was held, is a large burr oak tree, which looks as though it might have stood here for many centuries. At the root of this tree, said the old man, Pontiac (or the Indian who passed for such) was sitting, when a warrior came up behind him and split his head open with a tomahawk ·

of friendship was given to me at Greenville by
your great chief (General Wayne). On it you
see the face of our great father at Washington,
and as long as this hangs from my neck I never
will raise my tomahawk against the whites."

Pledges of friendship were made by the chiefs,
and Governor Edwards dismissed them with many
presents, when they returned to their homes.
For several months after this council harmony
between the Indians and frontier settlements was
undisturbed, and people passed back and forth to
Lake Michigan, as in former days.

About the first of August two emisaries from
Tecumseh arrived on the Illinois river informing
the Indians that war existed between the United
States and Great Britain, and tried to induce
them to take part with the latter. A council was
called at Gomo's village, at which the chiefs of
the different bands opposed taking part in the
war. On the following day about one hundred
and fifty young warriors belonging to different
villages, left for Chicago, to join other bands in
an attack on Fort Dearborn. Black Partridge
on learning this fact, mounted his pony and followed these young bloods to dissuade them from
their purpose, but failed in his mission, and
a few days after their arrival at Chicago, the fort
was abandoned and troops massacred.

CHAPTER XVII.

TROOPS MARCHING AGAINST THE INDIANS.

In the fall of 1812, an army of two thousand mounted riflemen from Kentucky, under the command of General Hopkins, arrived at Fort Harrison on the Wabash. These troops were ordered by the commander-in-chief of the western army to march against the Indians on the Illinois river, as it was believed that many of them participated in the Chicago massacre, which had taken place a few months before.

On the 14th of October this grand army, the largest that had ever been so far west, entered Illinois in what is now Edgar county, and shaped their course northwest across the prairies. On the fourth day out the prairie was discovered on fire, and the soldiers became alarmed, fearing that they would be burned up in the flames. Being stricken with a panic they mutinied — all their patriotism vanished — and they resolved to go no further through a country enveloped in fire and

smoke.   While this great army was in confusion,
soldiers remonstrating with the officers, it is said
one Major Prunk rode up to General Hopkins
and ordered him to turn back.   The general
finding all military law at an end, abandoned the
expedition, and marched his army back to the
Wabash.

About this time Governor Edwards, with three
hundred mounted rangers, under the command
of Colonel Russell, marched northward from Fort
Russell, near the present site of Edwardsville, for
the purpose of operating with Hopkins' army
against the Indians.   But being unable to find
the army under Hopkins, they continued on
their way toward the Indian country.   Governor
Edwards' rangers being mounted on good horses,
without baggage except what each man carried
in his saddle bags, enabled them to march direct
for Peoria Lake, and on the fourth day reached
Black Partridge's village.   The Indians having
no warning of the approaching enemy, were un-
prepared to make a defense.   Most of the
warriors being off on a hunt, the squaws and
pappooses fell an easy prey to the rangers.   The
Indians, panic-stricken, fled from their village,
leaving in their flight ponies, camp equipage and
all other valuables.   A few of the warriors were
wounded in the assault, so they could not make

their escape, and therefore became victims of the
assailants.   These wounded warriors with a number of pappooses and a few persons decrepid by
age, were killed by the rangers, who afterwards
said in justification of this barbarous act that
they did not leave home to take prisoners.

The village with all its contents was destroyed
by fire; even the corn in the caches was taken
out and burned, and many of the ponies were
taken off as trophies of war.

As soon as the rangers had completed their
work of destruction, they started back on a
forced march for the settlement, as they were
now in the midst of the Indian country, where a
thousand or more warriors could be raised in a
day's time.*

BLACK PARTRIDGE.

This chief, whose Indian name was Mucketey-
pokee, lived at his village on the bank of Illinois
river, a short distance above the head of Peoria
Lake.   Here he lived, and here he died, and in
the early settlement of the country, his grave

| |* There are conflicting accounts relating to the destruction of
Black Partridge's village, some of which contradict these barbarous acts of the soldiers. But I obtained my information
while in conversation with General Whitesides, who was present and participated in this affair. General Whitesides (then
a young man,) belonged to Captain Judy's company of spies.

was pointed to strangers. Persons are now living who knew this chief well, and from whom I
obtained a description of his person, and many
incidents relating to his life and character.

Black Partridge was tall and slim, with a high
forehead, a large nose, a sharp visage and piercing black eyes. His appearance was noble, his
form erect, and his figure commanding. The
long coarse hair, once as black as a raven, but of
latter years mixed with gray, hung in matted
clusters over his shoulders. On his breast he
wore a silver medal, on which was the medallion
head of General Washington, and in his nose
and ears were large gold rings.

In the border wars of Ohio, Black Partridge
took a part and with a few of his braves fought
against the whites. He was present and signed
the treaty of Greenville, in the year 1795, and
received from the hand of General Wayne, the
medal above referred to. This medal as an
insignia of peace and friendship, was carried about
his person for seventeen years, and surrendered it
to Captain Heald, August 15, 1812.

and had a good opportunity of observing what transpired. He
described some acts of the soldiers, which for the sake of humanity ought not to be recorded in history, and therefore will
bear no part in this narrative.

  Having already published some items in relation to the destruction of Black Partridge's village, it becomes unnecessary
to repeat them here.

On the morning of the Chicago massacre, Black Partridge entered the quarters of Captain Heald, the officer in command of Fort Dearborn, and said to him, " I have come to deliver up to you this medal which I have long worn as a token of friendship, and it is with a sorrowful heart I now part with it. But our young braves are resolved on imbuing their hands in human blood ; I cannot restrain them, and I will not wear an emblem of friendship while I am compelled to act as an enemy."

In Mrs. Kinzie's account of the Chicago massacre is related an incident of Black Partridge saving the life of Mrs. Helm, wife of Lieutenant Helm, second officer in command at Fort Dearborn. This incident almost rivals romance, but its truth is confirmed by a person still living— Mrs. Benson—who was present, and from whom I partly obtained the following narrative.

On the morning of the 15th of August, 1812, the sun rose with unusual splendor, and its golden rays were reflected from the smooth water of Lake Michigan, but many of the inmates of Fort Dearborn who then looked upon it, did not live to see it set beneath the western horizon.

At nine o'clock the troops left the fort in military array, with martial music, and flags flying. Captain Wells, having his face blacked after the

manner of Indians, and with his Miami warriors
mounted on horses, led the van. The troops on
foot followed, and next to them were the baggage
wagons containing the sick, with the women and
children, while the Pottawatomie warriors five
hundred in number, brought up the rear. This
caravan followed the road along the beach of the
lake for about a mile and a half, to a range of
sand knolls.* Here the Pottawatomies left the
road, and took to the prairie, when Captain
Wells, with his horse on a gallop, rode back and
told the troops to form for battle, as the Pottawatomies were about to attack them. Soon the
fight commenced, and the soldiers defended
themselves manfully, selling their lives as dearly
as possible, but many fell on every hand by an
overpowering enemy. Mrs. Helm, wife of Lieutenant Helm, then but seventeen years of age,
having been thrown from her horse at the com-
mencment of the fight, stood spell bound, looking on the scene of blood and carnage around
her. Her father and husband were engaged in
the fearful strife, and she expected every moment
to see them fall by the murderous savages. Soon
a warrior with an uplifted tomahawk approached

---

* This range of sand knolls was where Fourteenth street
strikes the lake, and were a kind of a land mark thirty years
ago, but have since been graded down in making the street.

her, but dodging to one side the blow intended for her head took effect in the shoulder, producing a ghastly wound. She caught the savage around the neck, and attempted to get possession of his scalping knife which hung in a scabbard on his breast, but the warrior threw her to one side and was about to use his tomahawk on her head, when she was caught in the arms of another Indian who bore her off, struggling, into the lake. Here she was plunged under the water, but her head was frequently raised, so she soon discovered that the Indian did not intend to drown her. On looking into the face of her captor, she recognized Black Partridge, the white man's friend, notwithstanding he was disguised by paint. When the fight was over her protector conveyed his charge to the Indian camp, and delivered her over to a friendly squaw who dressed her wounds.*

About two months after the events above narrated, Black Partridge learned that Lieutenant Helm, the husband of the woman whose life he had saved, was still a prisoner among the Indians at a village on the Kankakee river. On receiving this intelligence he boarded a canoe and went to Peoria to consult with his friends in relation

* This Indian encampment was on a small stream or slough, which ran along the line of State street, and entered the river near Clark street bridge. This camp, according to the statement of Billy Caldwell, was near where Jackson street crosses State.

to the Lieutenant's ransom. Captain J. B. Maillet, Antoine Des Champs and Thomas Forsyth, were consulted, and it was agreed by them that Black Partridge should go immediately to the Indian village and purchase the release of Lieutenant Helm. Presents were furnished by the three traders as a ransom for the prisoner, with a written order on General Clark, Indian agent at St. Louis for an additional one hundred dollars on his arrival there.

Black Partridge being provided with presents, and accompanied by a half-breed from Peoria, mounted their ponies and started on their mission of mercy. On arriving at the Indian village, they found Lieutenant Helm closely guarded by his captors, and suffering from a wound which he received at the massacre. When the old chief entered the lodge, Lieutenant Helm threw his arms around his neck and cried like a child. He knew that Black Partridge had rescued his wife, and saved the life of his father-in-law (John Kinzie) with his family, and in him he saw a prospect of his own rescue.*

---

* The wife of Lieutenant Helm was a step-daughter of John Kinzie, an Indian trader, who came to Chicago in 1804. Kinzie was a half-brother of Thomas Forsyth, of Peoria, and father-in-law of Mrs. Kinzie, who published a book on the early history of Chicago.

The wife of Captain Heald was a sister of Captain Wells; the latter was raised among the Indians, adopted their dress, customs and language, and lost his life at the Chicago massacre.

Black Partridge called the chiefs and warriors together and laid the presents before them, saying all these articles should be theirs, with an additional one hundred dollars in silver if they would send their prisoner to General Clark at St. Louis. After a long parley the Indians rejected the proposition, contending that the ransom offered was not sufficient.

A short time before Captain Heald had been a prisoner at this village, and the Indians sent him to St. Joseph in charge of three warriors, to be liberated, but the pay received in exchange for him was so small that the warriors were sent back to reclaim their prisoner, but Captain Heald having been sent to Detroit they failed to get him.

The Indians refused to release Lieutenant Helm unless the ransom was increased, so Black Partridge offered them his pony, rifle, and a large gold ring which he wore in his nose. This proposition was accepted, and Lieutenant Helm, with the half-breed, accompanied by a petty chief, all mounted on ponies, started the next day for St. Louis.

It was thought best to take the prisoner to St. Louis to be set at liberty, as the Indians might think if brought to Peoria that the French were in league with the Americans, and thereby create a feeling against them.

Black Partridge accompanied Lieutenant Helm

and his conductors one day's journey on their
way, and then started across the country for his
village on the Illinois river.

It was late at night, very dark, and the rain
pouring down in torrents, as the old chief, on foot
and alone, plodded his way through the thick
river timber toward his home, where he expected
to be warmly greeted by his family and friends,
but was doomed to disappointment.   The village
had disappeared—not a lodge nor a human being
could be found—nothing remained on its site but
the charred poles of which the lodges were constructed.   A pack of hungry wolves which had
been feeding on dead bodies, ran away at his
approach, and their howling during the night
added gloom and terror to the surrounding scene.
Black Partridge drew his blanket around him,
and with a sorrowful heart seated himself on the
ground to await the approach of day.   Next
morning he found among the dead his favorite
daughter, with her infant son clasped in her arms,
both stiff in death.   On the site of the village,
and in the swamp near by, he found the remains
of many of his friends, among whom was an old
squaw of ninety winters.

INDIANS ATTACKING THE SETTLEMENTS.

After the destruction of Black Partridge's vil-

lage, his band left the Illinois river, some of
whom found refuge on Bureau creek and others
on Green river, where they remained until the
following summer.   A party of warriors, headed
by Black Partridge, returned to the village some
days after it was destroyed, for the purpose of
burying the dead, and found their remains partly
devoured by wolves.   The warriors engaged in a
winter hunt, according to their custom, but Black
Partridge traveled over the country, visiting different villages, and holding council with their
chiefs in order to enlist them in his cause.   He
was now old—his head whitened by the snows of
seventy winters—still his figure was erect and his
step firm.   Age had not dimmed the fire of his
eyes, nor destroyed the ambition of his youth.
He had long been a friend to the whites, and had
done everything in his power to prevent the massacre at Chicago.   He had saved the life of Mrs.
Helm, at the risk of his own, and had collected
around him a few faithful friends to guard the
house of John Kinzie, and thereby rescued his
family as well as other prisoners from massacre.
He had traveled a long way to the Kankakee
village, and given his pony, rifle and ring to ransom Lieutenant Helm, and while tired and
hungry he returned to find his home desolated,
and his friends murdered or driven away.   Not-

withstanding Black Partridge had done all this,
the whites made war against him, burned his
town, destroyed his corn, carried off his ponies,
and killed about thirty of his people, among whom
were some of his kinsmen, and he now lived only
for revenge.

On the following summer Black Partridge.
with about three hundred warriors mounted on
ponies, left for the frontier settlements in the
southern part of the State. They went within
thirty miles of the settlement, and secreted themselves in the thick timber of Shoal creek, now in
Bond county. From here they sent out small
war parties to attack the settlers and kill defenseless women and children. The people were
greatly alarmed at these depredations; many fled
from their homes and sought safety at Cahokia
and Kaskaskia; others built temporary forts to
shield themselves from the tomahawk and scalping knives of these ruthless savages. It is said a
half-breed, dressed as a white man, acted as a spy,
visiting different settlements and informied the
Indians of the most exposed points. Through
this spy the Indians learned that an expedition
was about to be sent against their villages on the
Illinois river, so they broke up their camp and
left for their homes.

CHAPTER XVIII.

While the inhabitants of Peoria were quietly pursuing their daily avocation of farming, hunting and trading with the Indians, being as they supposed at peace with all the world, a plot was laid for their destruction. Being located in the midst of a wilderness country, two hundred miles from the nearest American settlement, and having but little intercourse with the civilized world, they would not have known that war between the United States and Great Britain existed if they had not learned the fact from the neighboring Indians.

Although the French at Peoria had lived within the jurisdiction of the United States government for thirty-four years, they had never taken the oath of allegiance, acknowledged its power, nor paid tax to its support. They were a foreign people, speaking a different language, with habits and customs peculiar to themselves, and all their trade and intercourse was with the French citizens of Canada.

The residents of Peoria had taken no part in the war, as it was afterwards proven, but nevertheless they were charged with assisting the Indians by supplying them with arms. Report said that they were bringing munitions of war from Canada, and selling them to the Indians to enable these savages to make raids on the frontier settlements. It was also alleged that they had sent five horses over to the Sac village, near Rock Island, to pack lead for the Indians, and this lead was paid for in goods furnished by Peoria merchants. But the most damaging of all the evil reports in circulation, and which caused the greatest feeling of resentment among the people, was that of cattle stealing. It being reported and believed by people everywhere that Captain John Baptiste Maillet, the chief military man of Peoria, with a number of followers had been stealing cattle from the Wood river settlement, in Madison county, to feed the Indian army then collected at Gomo's village. These reports were afterwards shown to be false, and instead of Captain Maillet being a cattle thief, as reported, he was rewarded by an act of Congress for his loyalty to the United States government.

The evil reports in circulation about the French

at Peoria were generally believed, and Governor Edwards, supposing they were true, called for volunteers in order to send an armed force against them. About two hundred men responded to the call, who were placed under the command of Captain Craig, and rendezvoused at Shawnee-town. Four keel-boats were prepared, with rifle ball proof planking, mounted with cannon, and filled with armed soldiers. These boats left Shawneetown early in October, and arrived at Peoria on the 5th of November. The inhabitants of Peoria were much surprised to see four armed boats land at their wharf, as no large craft had ever reached that place before.

The following account of the arrival of these boats, and the burning of Peoria, are principally taken from the statements of Antoine LeClair and Hypolite Pilette, who were present, the latter being a boy at the time. LeClair was a half-breed, and acquired much celebrity in after life as the proprietor of Davenport, Iowa. Pilette is now living on the American Bottom, near Prairie de Rocher, and to whom previous refer-ence has been made.

BURNING OF PEORIA.

On Sunday morning, November 5th, 1812, as the people of Peoria were assembled at church,

engaged in saying mass, they were startled by the
report of a cannon. The congregation, partly
through fright and partly by curiosity, ran out of
the church, when they discovered four armed
boats in the lake under full sail. On coming opposite the town, the boats rounded to and landed
at the wharf. Father Racine came down from
the pulpit, and in his long black robe, with his
bald head uncovered, started for the landing, followed by all his congregation, men, women and
children. Here they were met by Captain Craig
and some of his men, who had landed from the
boats. Thomas Forsyth, who spoke English, inquired of the commanding officer, Captain Craig,
the object of his mission, but he evaded answer-
ing the question, and in return demanded of the
citizens a supply of meat and vegetables for his
men, which were furnished them.

The soldiers landed from the boats and scattered
through the town in search of plunder, and committed many depredations on the people. They
broke open the store of Felix Fontain, in which
Antoine LeClair was a clerk, and took therefrom
two casks of wine, and drank their contents.
Many of the soldiers got drunk, forced their way
into dwellings, insulting women, carrying off
eatables, blankets, and everything which they
took a fancy to. It was long after dark before

Captain Craig succeeded in getting his drunken disorderly crew on board, when the boats were pushed off from shore to prevent further depredations on the citizens. The boats lay at anchor off in the lake in order to prevent the soldiers from again visiting the town, as well as a precaution against an attack from the Indians.

During the night a high wind arose, and to escape the waves in the lake the boats raised their anchors and dropped down into the channel of the river, about one-half mile below the town, where they remained until morning. About daylight, eight or ten guns were fired in quick succession in the thick river timber close to the boats. Captain Craig thinking that they were attacked by Indians, ordered the boats to push out into the channel of the river, while the cannons were brought to bear and several shots fired into the timber in order to dislodge the supposed Indians.

About daybreak on the morning of the supposed attack on the boats, a party of French at the village, consisting of eight or ten in number, went out in the river timber to shoot some beeves. The cattle being mixed with buffalo would live during the winter without feeding and became partly wild, so they were frequently hunted down in the woods the same as deer.

This party of hunters had attacked the herd in their lair, near where the boats of Captain Craig were at anchor, shot three beeves, and had commenced skinning them when the 'timber was riddled with cannon shot. The hunters became frightened, left their beeves undressed, and in great haste returned to town without having the slightest idea from what cause these hostile demonstrations were made by the troops.

A council of war was held among the officers, all of whom were in favor of burning the town, and taking the men prisoners of war, as they had without doubt, pointed out the location of the boats to the Indians, and therefore were accessory to the attack. The boats were run up to the town, when Captain Craig, with an armed force visited each house and took all the heads of families prisoners. Some of the men were still in bed, and not allowed time to dress, but hurried off to the boats with their clothing in their hands. A torch was applied to every house, and these with their contents were burned.

Women and children, with wild screams escaped from the burning buildings, and like a herd of frightened deer collected on a vacant lot back of the town. The church, which contained a golden image and a crucifix, with other valuable religious emblems, a present from the Bishop of

Quebec, was burned. The wind-mill, which stood on the bank of the lake and filled with grain and flour belonging to the citizens, was burned, as well as stables, stock-yards, corn-cribs, &c.

Felix Fontain, Michael LaCroix, Antoine Des Champs and Thomas Forsyth, all of whom were traders, with their stores filled with goods, which was consumed by the flames. An old man named Benit, formerly a trader, who had saved a large amount of gold by the toil of half a century, which he had laid away for old age. This gold was secreted in his dwelling, but finding it on fire he rushed in to save his treasure, and perished in the flames, and his bones were found among the ashes on the following spring by a party of hunters who visited Peoria. Mrs. LaCroix, a lady of refinement and of great personal attraction, who in after years became the wife of Governor Reynolds, being alone with four small children when her house was set on fire, appealed to the soldiers to save the clothes of herself and little ones, but her appeal was in vain, and with her children only she escaped from the burning building.

There is an incident connected with the burning of Peoria which to some extent explains the barbarous conduct of the soldiers, and somewhat palliates this offense against humanity. About

two months before Peoria was burned, General
Howard, then stationed at Portage du Sioux, sent
one of his soldiers, a young half-breed named
Snipkins, to Peoria, in order to ascertain if the
French were assisting the Indians in carrying on
a war against the settlements, as had been reported. This messenger, by courtesy, was called
Howard's express, but in fact was a spy, learning
all he could from the citizens without letting his
business be known. This young scapegrace, instead of returning to the army and reporting the
true state of affairs, according to orders, became
enamored with a girl and prolonged his stay until
the arrival of Captain Craig. And to escape punishment for disobeying orders, he reported to the
troops under Captain Craig that he was detained
by the people of Peoria against his will, being a
prisoner in their hands, which was afterwards
shown to be false. If this messenger had returned to the army, and reported as he was ordered
to do, Craig's expedition would have been abandoned, and the destruction of Peoria averted.

A short time before Peoria was burned, Thomas Forsyth was appointed a government agent,
but this appointment was kept a secret by the
department at Washington, as it was thought, if
known, it would lessen his influence with the Indians, and probably prejudice his townsmen

against him. When Forsyth was made a prisoner he showed his commission under the United States seal to Captain Craig, but the incredulous captain pronounced it a forgery.

When the destruction of Peoria was completed, the boats started down the river on their return homeward, carrying with them all the men as prisoners of war. Two miles below the present site of Alton, in the thick river timber, these prisoners were set at liberty, without tents, provisions, or means of returning to their families.

The women and children having been left at the burned town without food or shelter, were therefore in a suffering condition, and without assistance they could not be relieved from their helpless situation. It was now late in the fall, the sky overcast with gray clouds, and the cold November winds howled through the forest trees. With high winds were squalls of snow, and the roaring and lashing of waves in the lake caused mothers to draw their infants closer to their bosoms to protect them from the inclement weather. To these destitute helpless beings all was dark and cheerless; the lamentations of mothers and cries of children were heard far away, and touched the heart of a sympathizing friend, although a savage. While in the midst of trouble they discovered a lone Indian walking leisurely along the beach of the lake, and with a firm step approaching them. He carried a rifle on his shoulder, a tomahawk and scalping knife in his belt, and his face was painted in many colors. Notwithstanding he was disguised by paint, they recognized in the approaching Indian Gomo, a friendly chief, who had a village where Chillicothe now stands.

On the approach of Captain Craig's forces, the inhabitants of Gomo's village fled from their homes and secreted themselves in a thick grove of timber a few miles west of the river. But Gomo, with two of his warriors, remained in the heavy timber near the lake watching the movements of the soldiers, and when the boats departed down the river they came forth from their hiding place to assist their friends in distress. Gomo and his warriors furnished provisions and shelter for the destitute women and children, and provided them canoes (those belonging to the French having been destroyed by the soldiers,) to descend the river. When supplied with an outfit for the journey, the women with their little one started down the river, camping each night on its banks, without tents or shelter from the cold night air. After many days of hardship and exposure, drenched by rain and suffering from cold, they reached Cahokia, where they were provided for by their countrymen, and afterwards joined by their husbands and fathers.

It has been stated that Captain Craig took the women and children on the boats with the men, and set them all at liberty on the east bank of the Mississippi river. But this is incorrect, as the report applied to a few families only. The family of Thomas Forsyth, and perhaps one or two others were taken on the boats, but I am informed by Rene LaCroix and Hypolite Pilette, who were present, (being boys at the time,) that the families to which they belonged, with many others, went down the river to Cahokia in bark canoes furnished by the Indian chief Gomo, as previously stated.

Captain Craig has been greatly villified for burning Peoria, but it must be recollected that he acted under the orders of Governor Edwards, who approved of his conduct, and afterwards appointed him to an important office.

It appears Governor Edwards was misled by false reports, which caused him to make war on innocent people, and therefore should not be censured for doing that which he believed, at the time, to be his duty.

CHAPTER XIX.

DESCENDANTS OF FRENCH SETTLERS AT PEORIA.

The descendants of the French who were born at Peoria, only three are now living, and they of course are far advanced in life. I visited these persons, and listened to an account of their early recollections of Peoria, as well as the traditions of their ancestors. One of these descendants, Robert Forsyth, lives on a farm in Missouri, six miles west of St. Louis. He is a son of Thomas Forsyth, who was a trader at Peoria, and held a commission of an Indian agent from the government when the town was destroyed. After the destruction of Peoria, Forsyth was appointed an agent for the Sacs and Foxes at Rock Island, and held that position for many years. He was one of the claimants for the land on which Peoria stands, and his son Robert, (above referred to,) prosecuted these claims against the occupants, and realized a large sum of money out of them.

Rene LaCroix, another of the descendants, lives in Belleville, and like Forsyth obtained a large sum of money out of the French claims. His father, Michael LaCroix, a trader at Peoria, was on his way to Canada with a pirogue loaded with furs when the town was burned. While at Montreal he heard that the Yankees had burned Peoria and killed all its inhabitants, among whom were his wife and children. With his heart filled with revenge, he joined the British army, became an officer, and participated in many of the battles of the war. After the war was over, he learned that his family were still living, and at Cahokia, so he came west to join them. On the following year Mr. LaCroix died, and a young lawyer of Cahokia, named John Reynolds, afterwards Governor of Illinois, married his widow.

Hypolite Pilette is a son of Louis Pilette, one of the French land claimants, born at Peoria in 1799, and is now living on the American Bottom. He claims to be a great grandson of Captain Richard Pilette, who in the year 1686 built Le Fort Des Miamis, on Buffalo Rock, and has now in his possession the sword, eagle and epaulets worn by that distinguished personage.

While speaking of the burning of Peoria in 1812 by Captain Craig, he said : "On a cold November morning, when a boy of thirteen years of age, I was driven from home without coat, hat or shoes ; my mother sick with the ague, and with an infant in her arms, was compelled to leave her bed, protected from the cold winds only by an Indian blanket, while the house with all its contents was devoured by the flames.   My father a prisoner, my mother sick, my brothers and sisters almost naked, without food or shelter, and not a dwelling of a white man within two hundred miles.   Thus we were turned out of doors to starve and freeze, but fortunately were rescued by some friendly Indians."

Three days after Peoria was burned, Mrs. Pilette, with her children, were put in a canoe by the Indians, and with her family started down the river.   After six days of exposure, suffering from cold and hunger, they reached Cahokia, where they were provided for by their countrymen.

While speaking of the past, Pilette became much excited, his eyes flashed with anger, his voice was raised to a high key, and in broken English he denounced the barbarous acts of Captain Craig, and from that time to the present, said he " I hate Yankees."

MRS. BESSON'S NARRATIVE.

While in East St. Louis, I heard of an old

lady by the name of Mrs. Besson, who was one of the captives at the Chicago massacre, and is probably the only one now living. I called on this lady and listened to her narrative relating to this affair, which to me was very interesting. She said her early recollections were associated with Chicago river, Lake Michigan, and Fort Dearborn, by the side of which she spent many of her childhood days, and gathered flowers on the wild prairie, now covered by the great metropolis of the west. Her maiden name was Mary Lee, daughter of Charles Lee, who with his family came to Fort Dearborn soon after it was built. Their dwelling stood on the beach of the lake near the fort, and back of it was a small garden enclosed by a rail fence. For a number of years her father, Mr. Lee, was engaged in agricultural pursuits, selling the products of his farm to the garrison at high rates.

Mr. Lee made a large farm at a grove of timber on the south branch of Chicago river, four miles from its mouth, where Bridgeport is now located. The land near the lake, being either wet or sandy, rendered it unfit for farming purposes, therefore, it was necessary to go up the river to make a farm, where the prairie was more rolling and the soil rich. The communication between Mr. Lee's residence and his farm during the spring and summer, was principally by a canoe on the river, as the road connecting them crosses a flat prairie covered with water much of the time.

Mr. Lee built two cabins on his farm, and employed a number of persons to work the land. For some years the grove with its surroundings, was known as "Lee's Place," afterwards called Hardscrable, and it was here the Indians killed and scalped two persons, White and DeVow, on the 7th of April, 1812, an account of which is given in Mrs. Kinzie's early history of Chicago.

At the time of the Chicago massacre, Mr. Lee's family consisted of his wife, an infant two months old, his son John of sixteen years, Mary, now Mrs. Besson, the subject of our sketch, twelve, Lillie, ten, and two small boys.

When the troops left Chicago for Fort Wayne, Mr. Lee with his family accompanied them, taking with him all his horses, but leaving behind a large herd of cattle, which were on the following day shot by the Indians. Mrs. Lee with her infant and two youngest children were in a covered wagon, while the two girls were on horseback; and all followed the army along the beach of the lake, on their march toward Fort Wayne on the Wabash.

Little Lillie was a very hansome child, a great

pet among the soldiers and citizens about the fort, but she never before appeared so beautiful, as on the morning they left Chicago. She was mounted on a large gray horse, and to prevent her from falling off or being thrown, was tied fast to the saddle. She wore a white ruffled dress, trimmed with pink ribbon, a black jockey hat with a white plume on one side. As her horse pranced and champed the bits at the sound of martial music, little Lillie, in a queenly manner sat in her saddle chatting gaily with her sister Mary, who rode by her side. As the soldiers threw kisses at her she would return them in her merry glee, talking and laughing mirthfully with many of her acquaintances. Her young heart was made happy by the excitement of the morning, and had no warning of the awful fate that awaited her, less than one hour afterwards.

Soon the guns of five hundred savages were raised against the troops, and by their murderous fire a large portion of the brave band were stricken down.

During the battle, little Lillie was wounded and fell from her seat, but still hung by the cord which bound her to the saddle. While in this condition the frightened horse ran back and forth until he was caught by an Indian, and the child rescued from her perilous situation. When the battle was over Waupekee, a chief who had often been at Mr. Lee's house, and trotted little Lillie on his knee, was much grieved to see her thus wounded, as he loved the child as though she were his own daughter. On examining Lillie's wound and finding it mortal, the chief put an end to her suffering with a stroke of his tomahawk. Waupekee afterwards said, to tomahawk little Lillie, was the hardest thing he ever did, but he could not bear to see her suffering.

Mr. Lee and his son John were killed in the battle, and the two young children fell victims to the savages, while Mrs. Lee and infant, with Mary were taken prisoners of war.

Mrs. Lee fell into the hands of Waupekee, who had a village on the Des Plaines river, about twenty miles from Chicago. This chief treated his prisoners kindly, and tried to induce her to marry him, notwithstanding he already had three wives. But she declined the marriage proposition, hoping some day to be ransomed, and again restored to friends and civilization.

During the winter Mrs. Lee's child took sick, and after all the known remedies of the Indian doctor had failed to remove the disease, the chief proposed to take it to Chicago for medical treatment. A Frenchman named DuPin, had taken possession of Kinzie's house soon after the de-

struction of the fort, and here carried on a trade
with the Indians for a number of years.

On a cold day in the latter part of the winter,
Waupekee wrapped the sick infant in blankets,
mounted his pony and with his charge started for
Chicago. On arriving at DuPin's residence, Waupekee carefully laid his package on the floor.
"What have you there?" asked the trader. To
which the chief replied, "A young raccoon,
which I have brought you as a present." And
unwrapping the package there lay the sick infant,
almost smothered in the thick folds of the blankets. The trader made a prescription for the child,
after which the chief carried it back to its mother, and it finally got well.

The trader became interested in the welfare of
Mrs. Lee, and offered Waupekee a large amount
of goods for his prisoner. The offer was accepted, the prisoner brought to the trading house and
set at liberty. Soon after Mrs. Lee's liberation,
this lonely captive widow became Madam Du-
Pin.

In the division of prisoners after the battle,
Mary Lee was taken to an Indian village on the
Kankakee river, and on the following spring was
taken to St. Louis and ransomed by General
Clark, the Indian agent. Some years afterward
she married a French Creole by the name of Bes-

son, but is now a widow, living with a distant connection of her husband's. Mary never met her mother after that fatal day, and for many years supposed she was killed with the other members of the family, but subsequently learned of her captivity, liberation, marriage and death.

MISSIONARIES OF ILLINOIS.

In every French settlement of the west a Jesuit missionary preceded it, and much credit is due to them for preparing the minds of the Indians to the introduction of their countrymen. Many of these missionaries were talented and efficient bearers of the cross, who devoted their whole lives to the conversion of heathens. They traveled through all parts of the west, from Canada to New Orleans, sacrificing the comforts of civilization for the purpose of Christianizing the Indians.

As early as the year 1640, Father Nicollet, a French Jesuit priest from Canada, preached to the Indians within the limits of Illinois. This devout priest traveled through the lake country in advance of all other missionaries, preaching to the Indians and telling them the story of the cross. He visited Green Bay in 1638, and in all probability was the first white man that ever

rowed a canoe on the waters of Lake Michigan.
He passed down the west side of the lake to the
mouth of Chicago river, where he met a large
party of Illinois Indians, engaged in fishing.
Here Father Nicollet remained many days,
preaching to the Indians, some of whom were
converted and received baptism. At the mouth
of the river he raised a cross, and taught the Indians to look upon it when trouble and
misfortune overtook them, and through its efficacy all their evils would be expelled. The spot
where the cross was erected was hallowed by the
Indians, and pointed out to Marquette on his
visit to the place twenty-three years afterwards.

Father Nicollet lived ten years among the savages, without meeting a white man, and became
an Indian in dress, habit and language, still remained a zealous Catholic, but at last he returned
to civilization because he could not live without
the sacrament.

After Marquette, probably the most devoted
and successful missionary was Father Allonez,
who established missions in various parts of the
west. He came to America when a young man,
and spent a long life in preaching to the Indians,
and left his bones in the wilds of the west. He
established a mission at St. Mary's, one at Green
Bay, and one at St. Joseph, but the last and most

important ones were at Cahokia and Kaskaskia.

In the year 1632, Father Allonez and Father Hugues Pinet accompanied La Salle in his voyage to the mouth of the Mississippi, and they preached to the Indians at every village where they stopped. On the return of this exploring party, they halted several days at Cahokia, which at that time was a large Indian village. The natives supplied the voyageurs with corn and buffalo meat, and the best lodges in the village were provided for their occupation.

When La Salle's party were about to continue their journey, the Indians prevailed on the two priests to remain with them, and teach them the word of life. The devoted priests consented to remain, and set about Christianizing the heathens. They visited Kaskaskia and other Indian villages, baptizing a large number of warriors, and enrolled their names in the church book. The Indians everywhere welcomed the priests, listening to their teachings and doing their bidding. They learned the story of Christ's crucifixion, and with a trembling voice repeated it to their friends. They not only received baptism at the hands of the priests, but allowed themselves to be sprinkled with holy water, which they believed blotted out all their past sins and saved them from perdition.

For twenty years Father Pinet remained at Cahokia preaching to the Indians, but on feeling the infirmities of age he went to Fort St. Louis, where he died on the 15th of July, 1704, in the seventy-ninth year of his age. They buried him in the French cemetery on the river bank, at the west end of LeRocher, and over his grave was erected a large monumental cross hewn out of red cedar.

About the year 1814, an old man with long white hair, which hung in matted clusters over his shoulders, by the name of Wigby, appeared among the Indians, and for a number of years preached at different villages along the Illinois river. Nothing is known of this man's history, except that he had been for a long time among the Indians on the Wabash, and spoke their language well. It is believed that he was a Baptist, as he immersed all his converts, telling them that this was necessary for their admission into the happy hunting grounds beyond the skies.

Wigby lived at Senachwine's village, and was accompanied by that chief in all his ministerial labors among the different bands. Senachwine was baptized by him, and professed to be a Christian, but the missionary could not induce him to abandon polygamy and put away his many wives.

Four years after Wigby came to the country

he died, and was buried on a high bluff overlooking the village of Senachwine, and his grave was pointed out to some of the early settlers.

Among the energetic and successful Protestant missionaries of this country, was Elder Jesse Walker, of the Methodist denomination, who acquired great celebrity thoughout the west.   For many years Walker was engaged in holding camp meetings in the south part of the State, but in the year the 1824 he came north and established missions along the frontier settlements.

Elder Walker was a short, heavy-set man, very dark skin, walked erect, with an independent pompous bearing, and possessed great energy and force of character.   He was a bold undaunted missionary, bearing the standard of the cross triumphantly into the wilds of the west, among the red man as well as the white.

In 1826 Elder Walker established a mission school among the Indians at a place called Mission Point, on the Illinois river, a short distance above Ottawa.   He also established the first church at Chicago; died and was buried at Plainfield, about the time the settlement commenced there.

A Baptist missionary by the name of Adam Paine, preached among the Indians with great success, but was killed by them at the commencement of the Black Hawk war.

CHAPTER XX.

In September, 1813, General Howard left
Portage des Sioux on the Missouri river, with an
expedition against the Pottawatomie Indians.
His army consisted of five hundred regulars and
nine hundred volunteers ; the latter from Illinois
and Missouri. The regulars ascended the Illinois
river in keel-boats, while the volunteers being
mounted, crossed the Mississippi near the present site of Quincy, and marched through the wild
country to Peoria. On arriving at Peoria they
found it desolated, nothing remained of the old
French town except a few charred timbers, of
which the buildings had been constructed. No
Indians were seen here, but in the timber near
the outlet of the lake, there were signs of having
been a recent encampment of them.

The troops encamped on the old town site, and
a strong picket guard placed around the encamp-

ment to prevent being surprised by the Indians. During the night an alarm was given, and a report circulated through the camp, that they were about to be attacked by a large body of Indians. All the troops were under arms, many shots were fired at the phantoms, and one soldier killed by a sentinel, the alarm, however, was false, as no Indians made their appearance.

On the following day, the army went up to Gomo's village situated at the head of the lake, but found it deserted and no Indians were seen in its vicinity. After burning the town and destroying the corn in the caches, the army returned to Peoria and built a fort.

INDIANS COLLECT ON BUREAU.

Indian scouts discovered General Howard's army on its arrival at Peoria, and notified their friends at the different villages, of the fact. The inhabitants of Gomo's, Senachwine's and other villages, fled from their homes on being warned of their danger, and collected at Coma's village on Bureau creek. Here they intended to make a stand ; await the approach of the invading army, and fight for their country and homes. All the squaws and pappooses, with old warriors unable to bear arms, were sent up the creek about seven miles above the town, and there secreted them in the thick timber of the Bureau.*

At Coma's village were collected about one thousand warriors, occupying all the lodges; and the bank of the creek for a long distance was covered with camping tents. On the bottom prairie below the village hundreds of ponies were feeding, all of which were spanceled, so they could be caught and mounted at a moment's notice.

It was expected that Howard's army would follow up the river, and attack them in their retreat, so a suitable place was selected to make a defense. This was in the thick timber, some distance below the village, where they could fire on

* About two miles northwest of Princeton, in the valley of Bureau is a singular narrow ridge about sixty feet high, extending from the east bluff part way across the bottom. This remarkable ridge, which looks like a freak of nature, is known as the Back Bone, and along it now passes a public road. Among the Indians this place was a noted landmark, and it became equally so with hunters, in the early settlement of the country.

Immediately north of the Back Bone amid the thick bottom timber was an old Indian camping ground, and here their camp poles stood long after they had left the country. In the fall of 1836, a party of Indian hunters were encamped here for many days, and while in conversation with one of them, I obtained the following scrap of history :

"Many years ago when I was a small boy," said an Indian hunter, "four thousand squaws and pappooses were encamped on this very spot. Here they remained for many weeks secreted among the thick timber, so the army of whites could not find them." At that time all the warriors were at Indiantown, with the intention of fighting the whites if they came up the river in pursuit of them.

the invaders while crossing a small bottom prairie.

Indian scouts who were all the time on the alert, discovered troops ascending the river in keel-boats, and in all haste conveyed the tidings to the village. On receiving these tidings, the drums beat, Indians yelled, all was bustle and excitement, and soon the warriors were secreted in their ambuscade awaiting the enemy. But when they found that the boats continued on up the river, they returned to the village.

GUNBOATS ASCEND THE RIVER—LIEUTENANT ROBENSON'S PARTY.

Four keel-boats, mounted with cannon and filled with armed soldiers belonging to the regular army, under the command of Major Christy, ascended the river from Peoria in search of Indians. On landing at the different villages along the river, they found them deserted, all the Indians having fled from their homes. It was intended to ascend the Illinois as far as the mouth of Fox river, but finding it difficult to pass the rapids, they stopped at Starved Rock. On the following day the boats were turned down stream, landing at the mouth of Bureau creek, from here a party was sent out in search of Indians. About eighty soldiers, under the command of

Lieutenant Robenson, marched up Bureau creek with the intention of visiting Coma's village, located nine miles distant. After going six or seven miles up the valley, through thick timber with occasional bottom prairie, they discovered a trail filled with fresh poney tracks. On seeing these Indian signs, they came to a halt, and held a consultation on the propriety of proceeding further. Knowing that they were near a large Indian village, and at any point of timber were liable to fall into an ambuscade of lurking savages. Some were in favor of going on and burn the village if vacated, but fortunately a majority opposed it, consequently they turned about and retraced their steps to the river.

On the return of Robenson's command, who reported no Indians found, Major Christy came to the conclusion that they had fled from the country, he made preparations to descend the river. Before leaving, the cannons fired a salute, toasts were drank, and the stream named Robenson's river, which name it bore for many years afterwards, and so appeared on the early maps of the state.

Indian scouts had watched the keel-boats as they ascended and descended the river, and on seeing them land at the mouth of the creek and send out troops to make observations, they put their ponies on a gallop to convey the tidings to the village, and it it was the tracks of their ponies which Robenson's party discovered. On learning of the approach of the whites, warriors mounted their ponies, and rode with all haste to the place where they intended to attack the invaders. Here many of the warriors secreted themselves among the thick timber, while those mounted remained in the rear to intercept the vanquished troops. Had the soldiers under Robenson continued their march toward the Indian village, the probabilities are not one of them would have escaped from death, as the warriors out-numbered them ten to one, and many of them mounted, while the troops were on foot.

HOWARD'S ARMY ATTACKED BY INDIANS.

When the army under the command of General Howard arrived at Peoria, Black Partridge made an effort to unite the different bands, and thereby raise a large force to attack them before fortifications could be erected. Shaubena, Waba and Waubonsie, with many of their followers, were with Tecumseh on the Wabash, and the warriors of the different bands could not be united under any one chief. Senachwine was opposed to an offensive war, and being a chief of great influence and gifted with stirring eloquence, carried with him a large portion of the warriors. Black Partridge was grave and morose, brooding over the wrongs which he received from the whites the year before, and lived only for revenge. Notwithstanding he had taken many scalps the past summer, and murdered defenseless women and children, still he thirsted for more blood.

It was a beautiful clear day in the early part of Indian summer; the warriors were lounging along Bureau creek, some fishing, others running foot races, wrestling or playing with balls or hoops. All was quiet at the village, neither war dances, religious feasts, nor marriage festivals, nothing whatever to relieve the monotony of camp life. A party of warriors were about to start on a hunt, when two scouts arrived from Peoria, saying that the army was engaged in building a fort for the purpose of holding possession of the country. At this announcement Black Partridge, armed with a rifle and tomahawk, mounted his pony and rode back and forth through the camp calling for volunteers to follow him to victory. About three hundred responded to the call, among whom was a young brave named Autuckee, afterward head-chief at Indiantown, and known by many of the early settlers of this country. The warriors mounted their ponies, and before sundown were on their way to meet the enemy. Traveling part of the night they encamped in the river timber, about four miles above Peoria, and on the following day attacked the army. While the soldiers were engaged in building a fort, unconscious of danger, they were attacked by this body of Indians, and had it not been for persons outside of the picket guard giving timely alarm, in all probability a bloody battle would have been the result.

The following account of this affair is taken from the statement of Colonel George Davenport, who at that time, was a non-commissioned officer in the regular army, but in after years became a noted Indian trader at Rock Island.

A well having been dug within the stockades to supply the fort with water, it became necessary to have a sweep to draw it, so Mr. Davenport with two companions went into the woods to get a grapevine for that purpose. Having found one to answer the purpose, Davenport climbed the tree to cut it off, and while doing so he discovered a body of Indians skulking through the timber in the direction of the fort. On seeing their danger, Davenport and his companions fled towards the fort, but finding Indians in that direction they turned their course for the gunboats which were moored in the lake. With all their speed they ran for the boats, closely followed by the Indians, who fired at them yelling like demons. The men on board of the gunboats, being alarmed for their own safety, pushed them off from the shore, but fortunately one grounded on a sand bar, which was the means of saving the life of Davenport and his companions. The fugitives rushed into the water, waist deep, and pushed the grounded boat off and jumped on board of it. During this time the Indians were firing on then, and many of the balls whizzed by their heads, lodging in the side of the boat. The boats were now off some distance from shore, still the Indians continued to fire on them, but without effect. A cannon on one of the boats was brought to bear on the savages, but in the excitement of the moment its muzzle was raised above the port hole, and the ball tore off a portion of one side of the vessel.

The Indians attacked the fort, which was in an unfinished condition, but met with a warm reception from the soldiers. The cannon on the boat having been brought to bear on the savages, they abandoned the attack and fled for the timber, and on the following day returned to their village on Bureau creek.

BUILDING OF FORT CLARK.

Preparations having been made to build a fort

on the site of the old French town, for the purpose of holding possession of the country. Timbers were cut on the opposite side of the lake and floated across to build block and store houses, and enclose the fort with palisades. On a high piece of ground near the bank of the lake, and having a commanding view of it, they erected a fort. This fort was a simple stockade, one hundred and twenty feet square, constructed by placing in the ground two rows of split timbers, eighteen feet long, and filling the space between with dirt. A ditch surrounded the fort, and at two corners were bastions for mounting cannon. The fort stood with one corner to the lake, and at the southwest angle was a gateway, guarded by two heavy doors made out of split logs or puncheons. Inside of the stockades was a large block-house, two stories high, and on three sides of which were port holes so the inmates could fire on the enemy in case of an attack. Besides the block-house there were store-houses and quarters for the officers, and a number of small dwellings for soldiers.

When the fort was completed and the cannon mounted on its ramparts, with the flags waving on its bastions, General Howard ordered all the soldiers on duty, who formed in double file, fronting the gateway. A speech was made by the

commanding officer, the drums beat, the soldiers
cheered, the cannon fired a salute, and with much
enthusiasm the fort was dedicated, and named
Fort Clark in honor of General George Roger
Clark, the hero of Kaskaskia and Vincinnes.

With the army at Fort Clark was a Yankee
peddler, who acted as a sutler, by the name of
Jenkins, but on account of his close dealing acquired the cognomen of "Old Skinflint." He
was very unpopular with the soldiers, and all
efforts to beat him in trade had been a failure.
Among the volunteers was one John Murdick,
who was very fond of whiskey, but seldom had
money to buy it, so he put his wits to work in order to get some out of "Old Skinflint," as he called the sutler. Murdick placed in the bosom of
his hunting shirt two black bottles, one of which
was empty and the other filled with water. Taking out the empty bottle the sutler filled it with
whiskey, when Murdick replaced it in his bosom,
saying at the same time that he was out of money,
and it would have to be charged to him. The
sutler became angry, and after much parleying,
with many hard words on both sides, Murdick
consented to give up the whisky, but took out the
bottle containing the water, which "Old Skinflint"
emptied into the cask while Murdick walked off
with the whisky.

CHAPTER XXI.

A TREATY OF PEACE.

Black Partridge and his friends finding it impossible to unite the different bands, so as to prosecute the war successfully, thought it best to make peace, and accordingly a large delegation of chiefs and warriors went to Fort Clark for that purpose. When this party arrived within a few miles of Peoria, they came to a halt, and Senachwine, with two warriors carrying white flags, went forward to the gate of the fort and proposed to meet the commanding officer in council. Arrangements were made for a meeting on the following day, in a grove of timber above the fort, for the purpose of agreeing on terms of peace. At the appointed time about forty chiefs and warriors, decorated with wreaths of turkey feathers, made their appearance and were met by General Howard and all the officers of his command. After shaking hands and passing around the pipe of peace, Senachwine made a a speech before the council, in which he said that they had come to make peace with the whites, and bury the tomahawk forever. In reply to this speech General Howard said that he had no power to treat with them, but proposed to conduct their head chiefs to General Clark, superintendent of Indian affairs at St. Louis, who alone was authorized to make terms of peace. The Indians consented to this, and a delegation of thirteen chiefs and one squaw were selected to go to St. Louis. Among these chiefs were Black Partridge, Senachwine, Comas, Shick Shack and Gomo. General Howard ordered George Davenport to select four trusty men and escort these Indians to St. Louis.

All necessary arrangements having been made, this party on the following day went on board of a pirogue and started down the river for St. Louis. It being late in December, the weather cold, consequently after one day's journey the river froze up, and the remainder of the journey was made on foot. The pirogue was secreted in the thick timber, a short distance from the river, and each person carried with him a small quantity of provisions, leaving the remainder of their stores, including a keg of whisky, in a hollow tree, so they could be used on their return. At night both whites and Indians camped together, but each party kept a guard on duty, as they feared treachery.

This party after five days travel, arrived safe at St. Louis, a treaty of peace was concluded, and the Indians left five of their number at the garrison as a hostage for its fulfillment. The Indians on their return were escorted as far as Alton, above the settlement, and they returned to their homes.

After peace was made with the Indians, Fort Clark was abandoned, the troops returned to the settlement, and the volunteers were discharged from service.

WAUBONSIE

Was a chief among the Pottawatomies, and the leader of a small band consisting of about one hundred and twenty persons. It is said that he once had a village near the mouth of Fox river, but for many years he with his band made their home at Paw Paw Grove. Waubonsie was a large, fine looking Indian, tall and square built, with a hadsome face, an intelligent countenance, and in the latter part of his life became quite corpulent. He had an independent, pompous appearance, over-bearing towards his people,

and not very courteous to the whites, had it not
been for his color, dress and language, he might
have been taken for a thorough-bred Johnny Bull.
At the commencement of the Black Hawk war
Waubonsie was in favor of forming an alliance
with the Sacs and Foxes, and at a council held at
Indiantown in February, 1332, made a speech to
that effect. But being overruled by his people,
he professed to be friendly to the whites, joined
Atkinson's army at Dixon, and fought against
Black Hawk.

At the commencement of the British war,
Waubonsie was only a common warrior and went
with Shaubena to the Wabash, but was soon
after made a chief on account of the following act
of bravery: One day he left the camp to hunt
deer in the woods, and on coming near the Wabash river he heard the sound of voices. Approaching cautiously he discovered 'a party of
soldiers cordeling a boat up the river, loaded with
stores for Fort Harrison. To shoot one of the
soldiers and make his escape would have been
an easy matter, but this would not satisfy his ambition, as he could not in this way obtain the scalp
as a trophy. One man only was on the boat
steering it, while the other four were ahead with
a cordel line. As the boat came near the shore
Waubonsie jumped on board, tomahawked the

man at helm, took off his scalp, and with it made his escape. For this act of bravery he was made a war chief, and became the leader of a band.

In the summer of 1836 Waubonsie, with a few of his band came to Princeton, and bought of McCayga Triplett a beautiful spotted stallion of the Rocky Mountain breed, for which he paid three hundred dollars in silver, all in twenty-five cent pieces. Sometime afterwards, while the old chief was under the influence of whisky, mounted on his fine black and white horse, he rode back and forth through the town, putting on as much style as though he was a general in command of an army. To those around him he narrated (in bad English,) his many heroic exploits while fighting with Tecumsch, and told how many scalps he had taken with his own hands. From a pouch in his buckskin hunting shirt he drew forth two scalps, one of which the hair was red and the other black. The red one he said was taken from the head of a soldier at the battle of River Rasin, and the black one from a boatman on the Wabash.

In the fall of 1836 Waubonsie, went west with his band, and was never seen in this country afterwards. A short time after his arrival in the west, he was killed by a party of Sacs and Foxes for having fought against them in the late war.   His scalp was taken off, the body mutilated and left on the prairie to be devoured by wolves. The Sacs and Foxes made an attempt to kill Shaubena for the same offense, and for months haunted him down as though he was a wild beast.   To preserve his life he fled from the country, returning to his old home in Illinois, where he ended his days, but his son and nephew fell victims to these savages.

BURNING OF FORT CLARK.

It has already been stated, that Fort Clark was abandoned soon after it was built, and never occupied afterwards.   No white person lived at Peoria, (then known as Fort Clark,) after the troops vacated the fort until the spring of 1819.   The gate of the fort being left open, became a lair for deer and a roost for wild turkeys.   In the fall of 1816, a party of hunters from St. Clair county, came to Fort Clark and found about twenty deer in it.   The floor of the houses were covered with manure, and it also showed unmistakable signs of having been a turkey roost.   The hunters cleaned out one of the buildings and occupied it as a residence during a stay of ten days, while hunting deer and collecting honey in the river timber.   Fort Clark stood unmolested until the

fall of 1818, when it was burned by the Indians.
The following account of the burning of the fort
is taken from the statement of Colonel Gerden S.
Hubbard, now a resident of Chicago :

In the fall of 1818, Antoine Des Champs, general agent of the American Fur Company,
accompanied by a number of persons were on
their way to St. Louis, with two small boats
loaded with furs. On rounding the point of
the lake they discovered Fort Clark on
fire. On landing at the fort they found about
two hundred Indians engaged in a war dance,
celebrating some event which occurred in the late
British war. The warriors almost naked, hide-
ously painted, and as they went through the
dance yelled like demons. They had a large number of scalps hanging to their belts, and in óne
part of the dance these were placed on the end of
spears and held above their heads, after which
they would go through the motions of taking
them from the heads of their victims.

Des Champs was well acquainted with a number of the Indians, and he went among them,
engaged in conversation, leaving the boats guarded by one of his men and Mr. Hubbard, who at
that tine was a boy of only sixteen years of age.
The Indians inquired of Des Champs, who this
boy was, and in reply said that he was his adopt-

ed son from Montreal, but they did not credit
this statement, saying he looked like an American, and therefore regarded him with much
suspicion. An Indian took a scalp from his belt,
holding it near Hubbard's face, saying to him,
that he was an American and it was taken from
the head of his countrymen. Young Hubbard
became much frightened at these demonstrations,
and the Indian continued to annoy him by dip-
ping the scalp in the water, and with the long
hair sprinkled his face. In an instant all fear
vanished from young Hubbard, and picking up a
gun which lay in the bottom of the boat fired it
at the Indian, but as it went off the man in the
boat threw up the muzzle, thereby saving the Indian's life. This affair created great excitement,
and the Indians collected around the boat to ascertain the cause of it. Des Champs fearing
trouble, bid his Indian friends good-bye, went
aboard of the boat and continued on his way down
the river, camping on the opposite side some miles
below.

Although the buildings of Fort Clark and part
of the stockades were burned, as before stated, a
portion of the latter stood for many years afterwards. In the spring of 1819 a party of
emigrants from Clinton county, among whom
were Captain Abner Eads, Isaac and Josiah Ful-

ton and J. Hersey, came to Fort Clark, and from that time dates the first American settlement at this place. These emigrants pitched their tents against the stockades of the old fort, and for some years afterwards the enclosure within the pickets was used for penning work cattle. During the Black Hawk war in the summer of 1832, the old fort was repaired, new pickets put in place of those burned, and used by the people to protect themselves from the threatened attack of Indians.

One of the pickets of Fort Clark was still standing and perfectly sound as late as 1844, and attracted much attention as a relic of the past. It stood near the residence of Charles Ballance, Esq., who sawed off the top, put a ring in it, and used it for a hitching post. Afterwards this post was taken up by Mr. Drown, made into walking canes, and sold on speculation at fifty cents each. One of these canes is now in the possession of Samuel Sneed, of St. Clair county, who assisted in building the fort sixty-one years ago.

CHAPTER XXII.

IMMIGRATION OF POTTAWATOMIES

The following traditionary account of the immigration of Pottawatomies to Illinois was recently gathered from the tribe in western Kansas :

In the year 1769 the Pottawatomies of Ohio, Michigan and Indiana came west and took possession of the Illinois country. A village was built on Des Plaines river, and one on Sycamore creek. A chief named Wanesee who had acquired great fame in the Pontiac war, located a village at the mouth of Fox river. On the south side of the river opposite the outlet of Lake De Pue a village was built, but abandoned soon after for one on the north side of the lake.

An old chief named Wappe, with seven wives and about four hundred followers, located on Bureau creek, nine miles above its mouth, on the present site of Tiskilwa. For many years this village bore the name of its founder, afterwards Coma's village, but known by the early settlers as Indiantown. A chief named Tiskilwa lived here at one time, but little is known of his history except he had many wives and was a great hunter.

On the west side of the river near the mouth of Crow creek a village was founded by White Crow, who with his band came from the lake country. This chief died the same year the buffalo left the country, and a large mound, which is still to be seen, raised over his grave. In the early settlement of the country a chief named Crow lived here, from whom Crow creek and Crow prairie took their names.

The largest town on the river stood on the present site of Chillicothe, which was known in after years as Gomo's village. In the spring after the Starved Rock massacre, a chief by the name of Mucktapennesee or Black Bird with about five hundred followers came from the Wabash and located here. After the death of this chief his two sons were contestants for the chieftainship. Part of the band favored one and part the other. Failing to agree, one of the chiefs with a portion of the band located on the east side of the river at what was known in after years as Black Partridge's village. A few years afterwards these two chiefs with many of their warriors were killed in a battle with the Kaskaskia Indians.

West of the river on a small creek was an Indian village, the home of the celebrated chief Senachwine, but nothing is known of its early history.

POTTAWATOMIES OF ILLINOIS RIVER.

After the Illinois Indians were annihilated their conquerors took possession of the country and occupied it about seventy years. Between Peoria lake and the mouth of Fox river had long been known as the Indian country, and no part of the great west was so densely populated as this. Here lived the larger portion of the Illinoians, and here too were found their successors, the Pottawatomies. Although their towns and cornfields were mostly located on the Illinois river, they claimed as hunting grounds the country from the Wabash to the Mississippi river, and over this vast country they roamed at pleasure. In the year 1800 the commissioner of Indian affairs estimated that thirty thousand Indians (including all the different tribes) were living within the boundaries of this state, and about three-fifths of this number were on the Illinois

river. In the central portion of the state were a
few villages of Kickapoo Indians, who spoke the
same language as the Pottawatomies, and inter-
marrying with each other became as one people.
In the southern part of the state lived a large
band of Kaskaskia Indians, who were frequently
at war with the Pottawatomies, and raids were
after made into each other's country. For
many years a large tract of country laying between these tribes was overrun with game, as
both tribes were afraid to hunt there, being liable
to an attack by a war party of the enemy.

Sometime between the years 1785 and 1790
the Pottawatomies and Kickapoos attacked a war
party of Kaskaskians on Cash river, (now in
Johnson county,) and killed a large number of
them. Tradition points out the place where
this massacre took place, and in a cave near by is
still to be seen the bones of hundred of the slain.

On the 24th of August, 1816, a treaty was
signed at St. Louis between Governor Ninian
Edwards, General William Clark and Auguste
Chauteau, commissioners on the part of the
United States government, and twenty-eight Indian chiefs representing the Pottawatomies,
Ottawas and Chippewas. Twenty-three of these
chiefs were Pottawatomies, three Ottawas, and
two Chippewas. A number of Sacs, Foxes and

Kickapoo chiefs were present at this treaty, whose names appear as witnesses to the papers.

In this treaty, the Pottawatomies sold most of their lands, including all the country between the Illinois and Mississippi rivers, known as the Military Tract. This purchase extended north as far as the Indian Boundary Line, which ran from a point on Lake Michigan, south of Chicago, to the Mississippi river, near Rock Island. This line was surveyed in the summer of 1819 by John C. Sullivan, under the direction of Graham and Phillips, commissioners appointed by the President of the United States for that purpose. For a part of the way it divided the country between the Pottawatomies and Winnebagoes, and was made a standard line in the surveys of the state. In the year 1840 Wisconsin made a claim to that part of Illinois laying north of this line under the ordinance of 1787, and for some time it was a matter of controversy between the respective states.

Although the Pottawatomies had sold their lands, it was stipulated in the conditions of sale that they were to occupy them until required for actual settlement, and they gave them up only when the tide of emigrants obliged them to do so.

These Indians left the country at different times from 1832 to 1836, to occupy lands assigned them by the government on the west side of the Missouri river. But their trails across the prairies, and camp poles were seen here for many years afterwards.

Among the chiefs known by fur traders and early settlers, who died in this country and buried near their native villages, were Senachwine, Black Partridge, Gomo, Waba, Comas, and Shick Shack. Waubonsie, Autuckee, Meammuse, with other chiefs of less note went west with their respective bands. Shaubena went west with his band in the fall of 1836, but on the following year returned with his family to this country, and died on the bank of the Illinois river near Seneca, in the year 1858, and was buried in Morris cemetery.

Indians everywhere are attached to their home —the land of their nativity—but those on the Illinois river were unusually so. Their country was well supplied with game, and the groves filled with bee trees. Here were their sugar camps and the place of holding war dances and annual religious feasts. To their friends among the early settlers and fur traders, many of them with tears in their eyes expressed their regrets of leaving the home of their youth for a new one in a strange land.

For a number of years after the Indians left

this country, small parties of them were occasionally seen in the vicinity of their native villages, having returned for the purpose of once more looking on the scene of their youth, and the graves of their fathers. But soon their trails were fenced up by early pioneers, and the graves of their ancestors plowed over, so they ceased to return in after years.

It was intended to give a more elaborate account of the Pottawatomies of Illinois river, but the material is not at hand to do so. Many incidences relating to hunting parties, treaties, &c., are from tradition, others from Indian agents and fur traders, but they are found conflicting, and therefore bear no part in this work.

Col. Barassa, of western Kansas, an educated half-breed, with whom I have a personal acquaintance, has furnished many items relating to the Indians of Illinois river, some of which are given to the public, and others rejected as foreign to our purpose.

CEREMONIES OVER SENACHWINE GRAVE.

In the summer of 1831, Senachwine died and was buried on a high bluff, overlooking the village and surrounding country where his grave is still to be seen. A wooden monument was placed over his grave, and by its side was planted

a high pole, on which for many years waved a
black flag.   Two years after Senachwine's death,
his band left for the west, and are now living in
western Kansas.

In the summer of 1835, twenty-three warriors
with their heads decorated with turkey feathers,
and their faces painted in various colors, encamped on the site of Senachwine's village, while
their ponies were feeding on the prairie near by.
These warriors were sons and grandsons of
Senachwine, and had traveled about five hundred
miles to visit his grave.   With their faces blacked
and their heads covered with blankets, they knelt
around the grave invoking the Great Spirit to
protect the remains of the departed chief.   For
many hours they remained in this position, while
their wails and lamentations were heard far away.
After the mourning, came the dance of the dead;
which is described by an eye witness, Mr. Reeves
as very effecting.   The warriors divested themselves of their clothing, and smeared their bodies
with red paint, while on their cheeks and fore-
heads were many figures representing the sun,
moon and stars.   Their clothing, rifles, tomahawks
and scalping knives, were placed by the side of
the pole that stood at the head of the grave ;
and were now ready to commence the dance.
The warriors joining hands, dancing in a circle

around the grave, singing and chanting all the while. At intervals, they would stop dancing, the leader repeat a few words, when all would yell at the top of their voice; after which they would cry for a moment, and then continue the dance as before. When these ceremonies were ended the warriors mounted their ponies and left for their home in the far west.

A few days after the ceremonies, some person opened Senachwine's grave and robbed it of all its valuables, consisting of rifle, tomahawk, medals, &c., which were buried with him. The bones were also taken out and scattered around the grave, and bunch of long gray hair still adhered to the skull, giving it a ghastly appearance. Some days afterward a party of Indians belonging to Shaubena's band gathered up Senachwine's bones, reburied them, and placed the wooden monument again over his grave.

During the summer of 1835 James R. Taliaferro built a dwelling on the site of Senachwine's village, where he now lives. Mr. Taliaferro was present at the reburial of Senachwine's remains, and says that Indians from the west at different times made a pilgrimage to the grave. He also says that the pole stood at the head of the grave for many years, as well as the beaten path around it made by the dancing of warriors.

CHAPTER XXIII.

ATTEMPT TO MURDER A SURVEYING PARTY.

During the summer of 1822 the government surveys were completed in the Military District as far north as the Indian Boundary Line. At that time there was no settlement north of Springfield, and the country was full of Indians who still held it by the right of possession. Along Bureau creek were two surveying parties, one headed by Thomas C. Rector, and the other by Stephen Rector, with their camp on East Bureau, about one mile above its junction with the main creek. With these surveyors was a man named John Hanks, who was engaged as teamster, but spent much of his time in hunting and supplying the camp with meat. One night Hanks with two companions visited the Indian village, and making free with the squaws, became involved in a difficulty, and one of them received a wound by a tomahawk in the hand of an enraged Indian. One day while Hanks was

hunting deer in the creek timber, he encountered
a young Indian maiden, accompanied by two
small pappooses gathering flowers. Hanks made
overtures to the squaw when she ran towards the
village, but was caught and her person violated
by the hunter. On arriving at the village and
telling of her wrongs, the warriors were greatly
agitated, and some of them threatened to shoot
the culprit. A young warrior whose fancied bride,
was this young maiden, made preparations to
avenge her wrongs, and during the night, accompanied by about fifty of his friends, left for the
camp of the surveyors, with the intention of
killing the whole party as they lay asleep on their
bunks. Soon after they left, their murderous intentions became known in the village, when a drum
beat an alarm, to arouse the warriors from their
slumber. Autuckee, the head chief, with many
of his friends, mounted their ponies, and rode
with all speed, overtaking the would-be murderers before reaching the camp, compelling them to
return, and thereby saving the lives of the surveyors. The young warrior with a few of his
friends were kept under guard until the surveyors left the country.

KALTOO, OR YOUNG SENACHWINE.

On the death of Senachwine his son succeeded

him as chief of the band, and became noted among the early pioneers. His Indian name was Kaltoo, but was better known among fur traders as young Senachwine. He was an Indian of fine personal appearance, possessing excellent physical and mental powers, equal to his distinguished sire, but was affected with the demon of drunkenness. This young chief made frequent visits to trading posts along the river where he would spend days in dissipation, and sometimes get into trouble with the traders. While his band was encamped on the beech of the lake above Peoria, they held what is called a fish dance, and being well supplied with whisky, many got drunk, and while in the revelry one of the warriors killed another. Young Senachwine, accompanied by a number of warriors, took the murderer to Ottawa for the purpose of having him hung in accordance with the custom of the whites. On taking the murderer to the residence of Geo. E. Walker, then an Indian trader, but now of the Oriental Block, LaSalle street, Chicago, requested him to hang the culprit. Mr. Walker did not like to offend the chief, as he had a large trade with his band, so he consented to hang the prisoner, and prepared a rope for that purpose. When all was ready Mr. Walker said to young Senachwine that in a few months all the Indians of the different bands would be in Chicago to receive their annuities, and to prevent crime among tribes it would be better to hang him there publicly. But, said Mr. Walker, " I will hang the culprit now if you insist upon it." After some consideration the chief concluded to postpone the hanging until the meeting in Chicago, but before the time arrived the matter was settled among themselves, and Walker was not called on the second time to hang the murderer.

In the fall of 1841, ten years after the death of Senachwine, a lone Indian riding a jaded pony was seen on Green river, and for a few days was the guest of a half-breed by the name of Battis. This Indian, whose manly form, once the pride of his band, was now bent and palsied—not by age, for he was still in middle life, but by dissipation and disease. This Indian was Kaltoo, or young Senachwine of former days, whose handsome form and stately mien is still fresh in the minds of some of the few traders.

Kalto being afflicted with an incurable disease, and knowing that his end was nigh, left his home on Kansas river and alone visited this country in order that he once more might look on the haunts of his youth, and the grave of his father.

FUR TRADERS.

The fur trade on the Illinois river is so closely

connected with the French and Indians, that these sketches would not be complete without further allusion to it. For one hundred and thirty years, the French had undisputed control of the fur trade, and to them it was a great source of wealth. After the French were driven away from Peoria, there was but little trade on the Illinois river for the four succeeding years. The Indians in order to dispose of their furs, were obliged to carry them either to St. Louis or Chicago. At the latter place, a Frenchman by the name of DuPin, occupied Kinzie's dwelling, and for about four years carried on an extensive trade with the Indians.

In the year 1816, the American Fur Company established trading posts along the Illinois river, and monopolized the trade with the Indians for a number of years. One of these trading posts was near the mouth of the Kankakee river, one opposite the mouth of Bureau creek, and another a few miles below Peoria lake, at a place now called Wesley. This place originally was called Opa by the French, but afterwards known as the "Trading House," and for many years it was kept by a Frenchman, named Besson.

Antoine Des Champs, a Canadian Frenchman, long a resident of Peoria, but afterwards of Cahokia, was the first general agent of the American

Fur Company, and was succeeded by Gerden S. Hubbard. This company shipped their furs and pelts to St. Louis, in small Mackinaw boats called *bateau*, and by the same means brought goods up the river to supply the different trading posts. When emigrants came westward and settled on the Illinois river, it caused competition in the fur trade, and a few years later independent traders done the business of the country. Peter Menard established trading houses at different places in the Pottawatomie country ; John Hamlin, one at Peoria ; Thomas Hartzell, at Hennepin ; Simon Crozier, at the mouth of Big Vermillion, and George E. Walker, at Ottawa.

Shawnee Classics
A Series of Classic Regional Reprints for the Midwest